SR SUPPLEMENTS

Volume 19

Modernity and Religion

edited by William Nicholls

Published for the Canadian Corporation for Studies in
Religion/Corporation Canadienne des Sciences Religieuses
by Wilfrid Laurier University Press

1987

Canadian Cataloguing in Publication Data

Main entry under title:

Modernity and religion

(SR supplements ; 19)
Papers presented at the Consultation on Modernity
and Religion held at the University of British
Columbia, Dec. 15-18, 1981.
ISBN 0-88920-154-4

1. Religion – Congresses. 2. Religious thought –
20th century – Congresses. 3. Secularism –
Congresses. I. Nicholls, William, 1921 –
II. Series.

BL21.M63 1988   200   C88-093291-0

87 88 89 90 4 3 2 1

Cover design by Michael Baldwin, MSIAD

Order from:

Wilfrid Laurier University Press
Wilfrid Laurier University
Waterloo, Ontario, Canada   N2L 3C5

Printed in Canada

Contents

Contributors

Moshe Amon, Assistant Professor, Department of Religious Studies, University of British Columbia (to 1984).

Alan T. Davies, Professor, Department of Religious Studies, Victoria Campus, University of Toronto.

Robert S. Ellwood, Jr., Bashford Professor of Oriental Studies, School of Religion, University of Southern California.

Irving Hexham, Assistant Professor, Department of Religion, University of Manitoba (now Associate Professor, Department of Religious Studies, University of Calgary).

Shotaro Iida, Associate Professor, Department of Religious Studies, University of British Columbia.

Sheila McDonough, Professor, Department of Religion, Concordia University.

William Nicholls, Professor, Department of Religious Studies, University of British Columbia (Head, 1964-1983).

K. Dad Prithipaul, Professor, Department of Religious Studies, University of Alberta.

Tom Sinclair-Faulkner, Associate Professor, Department of Religion, Dalhousie University; Editor, *Studies in Religion/Sciences religieuses*.

Huston Smith, Thomas J. Watson Professor of Religion, Emeritus, Syracuse University.

John F. Wilson, Professor and Chairman, Department of Religious Studies, Princeton University.

INTRODUCTION

William Nicholls

The papers included in this volume were originally presented at the Consultation on Modernity and Religion held at the University of British Columbia, from December 15-18, 1981, under my chairmanship. Though extraneous factors have delayed their publication until now, the papers seem to be no less relevant than when they were originally delivered.

The idea of holding such a consultation originated in a seminar on the same subject which had been meeting regularly for several years under my chairmanship in the Department of Religious Studies of the University of British Columbia. The seminar consisted of the members of the department who were professionally interested in modern aspects of the religions we study. We hoped our studies and discussions might lead us to some understanding of modernity as a cross-cultural phenomenon. At the same time, we hoped that the relatively new discipline of religious studies might throw fresh light on a topic that had previously been the province of theologians and sociologists.

As more than one of us already knew from our own reading, theologians have devoted a great deal of thought to modernity. It would be possible to argue that the pivotal subject of debate among theologians for the past 200 years has been the relationship between modernity and the Christian tradition. Jewish thinkers since the Emancipation have encountered similar problems and proposed analogous solutions to them. In this sense our theme was certainly not a new one, and involved some traversing of well-trodden ground. These discussions had taken place, however, within Western culture. The newer academic study of religion is not confined to Western culture. Study of modernity in other cultures ought, we supposed, to lead to fresh understanding. The sociologists had also begun to study essentially the same phenomenon, under the name of modernization. The sociologists seemed to us more aware than the theologians that modernity, or modernization, is a world-wide phenomenon.

What then is modernity (a philosophical outlook or set of ideas?) or modernization (a social process?)? Since modernity evidently began in the West, is modernization identical with Westernization? Is modernity the same as secularity, as many theologians and sociologists in the West believe? If so, is modernization the same as secularization? Is its impact upon religion invariably weakening or destructive to the religious traditions? Are the responses of non-Western religious traditions to modernity modelled upon or analogous to those Western ones that have been studied already, or are they perhaps distinctive indigenous adaptations to the same world-wide development? After our seminar had been meeting for only a short time, it became apparent to us that widely different answers could be given to these questions. The co-operation of a broad spectrum of scholars from different disciplines and of different outlooks would probably be needed if answers were to be refined and developed to the point of commanding wide assent.

Thus the suggestion took hold of organizing a consultation of scholars interested in the field of modernity and religion to see what others were saying on our topic and to try out the ideas we ourselves were developing. A preliminary draft of the protocol of the consultation was circulated among some leading scholars, and their responses and critiques of our proposal proved sufficiently encouraging to go ahead with the practical problems of fund-raising, finding participants willing to read papers and discussion chairmen, and arranging the details of an actual program.

The consultation finally took place at International House on the campus of the University of British Columbia in fine December weather, and to our delight it came together as a coherent exploration of a common theme. The papers that were read provoked lively and suggestive discussions, and everyone got to know one another and their ideas quickly. Several of the leading participants afterwards told me that, from the point of view of their own work, this was one of the best scholarly meetings they had attended. There was also general agreement that this way of approaching the topic of modernity and religion was in fact a fruitful one and ought to lead to long-term research and continued communication between those engaged in it.

As editor of these published proceedings, I therefore have to hope that something of the vitality and stimulus of the actual consultation will be preserved in these pages. The papers presented here were not the whole of the consultation. Not only was each paper individually discussed at length, but the issues raised in each group of papers were also discussed in special sessions under the leadership of designated chairmen. It will be obvious that, for the participants themselves, such exchanges were of the greatest value. Nevertheless I am confident that the papers now presented to a wider public are worth studying in their own right, as a substantial body of research and reflection upon a topic of interest to anyone concerned with the present and future of religion.

The proposals for papers which we originally received seemed to fall into three main groups, which we designated "Identifying Modernity", "Case Studies," and "Modernity and Religion." While this general grouping of the papers has been preserved in publication, the order of the papers has been slightly changed, and some of them have been transferred to a different group in which they now seem to be more at home.

The papers by Huston Smith and Sheila McDonough were originally delivered without a manuscript, and have been revised for publication by their authors from transcribed tape recordings. McDonough's paper was originally an informal chairman's introduction to the discussion on modernity as a transcultural phenomenon. It was felt to contain material of such importance and interest that I asked her to turn it into a short paper for publication in this volume. Another stimulating paper is not included here because it has been published in a book which most readers of these proceedings are likely to have in their hands or can easily borrow. Jacob Needleman's paper on Socrates and the philosophical tradition can now be found in his The Heart of Philosophy (New York: Knopf, 1982). Sinclair-Faulkner's contribution has been newly written for these proceedings in an attempt to convey to the reader something of the content and flavour of the concluding discussions. The present introduction has also been newly written for this volume, replacing the informal chairman's introduction to the consultation.

All the authors have had an opportunity to revise their papers for publication, though most chose to make only minor changes. I undertook a small amount of editorial work, but have not shortened the papers or changed what was said at the time.

Several of the authors use the word "man," where it appears in a philosophical or theological context, in its traditional, inclusive sense. It is now a common practice, which is followed in publications of the Wilfrid Laurier University Press and of the Canadian Corporation for Studies in Religion, to change this term editorially to such expressions as "humanity" or "human beings." Although this could sometimes be done in the present volume, and inclusive personal pronouns substituted, it was not felt appropriate, in a work in which all questions concerning modernity were necessarily regarded as open, to make extensive editorial changes which might not have been faithful to the authors' intentions. Accordingly, in several chapters the usage of the word "man" and the corresponding pronouns must be understood to reflect the views of the authors, and not those of the Wilfrid Laurier University Press or of the Canadian Corporation for Studies in Religion.

The first two papers, by Wilson and Ellwood, address in rather
different ways the problem of the identification of modernity in the
context of religion. Wilson argues vigorously against reifying modernity, a practice cheerfully engaged in by several of the other participants (including myself; see p. 158). He believes that modernity is not
a distinct entity but a syndrome, in the original sense of the word, a
somewhat accidental combination of factors, some of the most important
of which, such as rapid social change, are not at all distinctive of
modernity. Part of his aim, therefore, is to achieve clarification at
the outset over what is to be understood by the term modernity, and if
possible to get future discussion to proceed on the basis of an agreed
upon definition. However, this was not achieved within the limits of
our own discussions. Nor did Wilson's view of modernity command general
assent. The reifiers went on reifying, and everyone discussed modernity
on the basis of their own explicit or implicit definition. Nevertheless, it seems that Wilson did not argue in vain, since subsequent contributors appeared to be more conscious of the definition of modernity
they were employing than might otherwise have been the case.

Ellwood's substantial paper immediately attracted a response, and
proved to be one of the focal points of the whole discussion. Whereas
several of the other contributors were interested in the impact of
modernity on traditional forms of religion, Ellwood was concerned to
describe in a more empirical fashion the character of modern developments in religious life, and to explain them by means of an anthropological analysis. In order to do so, he makes creative use of Redfield's
distinction between Great and Little Traditions in religion. Normally
found side by side, the Great Tradition is dominated by priests and
intellectuals, whereas the Little Tradition is characteristic of the
folk religion of Ellwood's title. He believes that modern religion in
its most lively and spontaneous forms is the contemporary form of the
Little Tradition, while the Great Tradition is in perhaps temporary
decline.

The next group of papers we designated, for want of a better term,
"case studies." Since they deal in somewhat more detail with specific
examples of modern developments in religion, they serve to provide some
of the empirical data on which future generalizations may eventually be
built. Davies, who is known for his work on antisemitism in Christian
theology, here turns to the rise of racist ideas in the nineteenth
century, seeing in their pseudo-scientific rationalizations of ancient
hatreds a significant symptom of modernity. Hexham's paper will be new

ground for many readers, as well as presenting a fresh view of its subject. Based on field work as well as on study of the (not very extensive) existing literature, his paper describes Afrikaner religion. He shows that, although often regarded as a modern as well as comparatively recent development, in many respects Afrikaner religion has preserved and even gathered to itself very old and often native African forms of religion.

Iida then considers the modern followers of the Buddhist prophet Nichiren, who lived in thirteenth-century Japan. He shows how Nicheren's teaching has been adapted to a period and a culture very different from its own to produce religious forms both strikingly modern and rooted in ancient tradition. McDonough deals with the Islamic reaction to Western modernity, choosing to concentrate, not on the Iranian revolution or Khomeinism, as it is beginning to be called, but rather on older and perhaps more central expressions of the horror of devout Muslims at the spiritual decline of the West. It is characteristic, she tells us, of the Islamic reaction to modernity to accept technology readily, but to shun as much as possible the secular culture that produced it, while awaiting the time when the spiritual decay of the West has proceeded so far that Western man will again turn to the ancient sources of his spiritual and cultural vitality, which Islam believes itself to have preserved unimpaired into our own time.

Two further papers, originally grouped with the case studies, now seem to fall more naturally into the final group, which had a more philosophical orientation. Amon's paper on utopias and counter-utopias evoked some of the most vigorous discussion of the whole consultation as a sort of limiting case against which others could measure their own views. As will be seen, Amon has very little hope for modernity, seeing it as thoroughly permeated with the utopian ideologies which in his view always have and always will generate counter-utopias of an increasingly destructive and demonic character. Against such modern utopianism Amon sets what he believes to be the perennial view of Jewish philosophy, that all the truth we need to know has been revealed to us, but in such a form that no one can ever justifiably claim to have understood it definitively. Debate, and some degree of tolerance for opposing interpretations, will therefore always be needed, and ideological certainty must be recognized as always a dangerous misunderstanding of the nature of truth. Such ideological modesty stands over against all modern messianisms, Jewish or otherwise.

Prithipaul's paper, written by a non-Western scholar who has lived in the West for a long time, expresses the profound disillusionment of a representative of an ancient, non-Western spiritual tradition when confronted by Western man's desertion of his own spiritual roots. He sees symptoms of this loss of roots in the failure of the modern enterprise of religious studies to come to terms with, or present credibly to its students, the Eastern spiritual traditions, which are in reality not essentially different from the tradition Western man has deserted.

Needleman's paper on the continuing relevance of the Socratic tradition in philosophy was also part of this group of papers. The reader may be referred to the remaining chapters of The Heart of Philosophy, which deal with matters of relevance to modernity and religion. The last two papers, by Smith and Nicholls, form a natural pair and were delivered in the same session. Realizing in advance that they held the most important of their convictions about the subject in common, the authors agreed to emphasize for the benefit of the discussion the matters on which they still differed. As in his recent books, Smith contrasts systematically the outlook of modernity with that of the philosophia or religio perennis. Modernity, whose basis is science, cannot deal with intrinsic values, with purposes or with meaning. This is not a problem arising from the newness or comparative immaturity of science: it is intrinsic to its method, without which it loses the rigour that gives it its validity in its proper sphere. The scientific outlook cannot accommodate transcendence. Only an ontological stance can do this, and modernity needs to adopt such a stance without abandoning the rigour of science in the sphere in which it is sovereign. Nicholls, in a somewhat different style, considers the existential or spiritual experience of living within modernity, characterized by the "death" or at least "eclipse" of God. He asks if the way forward is to be found by beginning with the paradoxical experience of "immanent transcendence," the transcendence of the ego by the observing Self — which may after all open up for us the way to other (traditionally recognized) dimensions of transcendence — without compromising modern man's autonomy and responsibility for his own spiritual destiny. These aspects of modernity are not to be surrendered out of any nostalgia for the glories of a religious past.

Finally, Sinclair-Faulkner, who had an important role as chairman of some of the concluding discussions, attempts to sum up from an independent standpoint the findings and implications of the consultation for future work. With the limitations and exceptions noted, this volume is now offered to the reader as the proceedings of the Consultation on Modernity and Religion of December 1981.

The consultation was made possible by grants from the Social Sciences and Humanities Research Council of Canada, the Alumni Association of the University of British Columbia, and the Faculty of Arts of the University of British Columbia. The publication of these proceedings was aided by a grant from the Vancouver Foundation, through the Faculty of Arts of the University of British Columbia, as part of its program of support for the humanities. The thanks of all the contributors, and of the participants in the consultation, as well as my own, are owed to these bodies. My warmest personal thanks are also due to Howard Steele, M.A., who acted as editorial assistant during my absence in 1984-85, to Carmen da Silva, who typed and retyped the manuscript not once but several times, and Olga Betts, who patiently saw the manuscript through the several stages of preparation of camera-ready copy.

These words are being written in the beautiful and holy city of Jerusalem, where I am spending a welcome leave of absence. Here, if anywhere on earth, the encounter between the religious traditions and the world of modernity can be experienced in its most vivid and urgent form. Perhaps some future consultation of this kind, building on our work in Vancouver, may one day meet in Jerusalem to take the questions we discussed a stage further. Be that as it may, our questions continue to press upon sensitive people, and every day that passes makes it clearer that our own time cannot be understood without some attempt to answer them.

February 1985

PART I

IDENTIFYING MODERNITY

MODERNITY AND RELIGION: A PROBLEM OF PERSPECTIVE
John F. Wilson

In this paper I will argue that the single most important objective for this conference ought to be to arrive at a hardheaded understanding of what we mean, or what we think we mean, by "modernity" in relation to culture. Energy directed to this task will be wisely expended and repay itself many times over. Failure to achieve adequate understanding of modernity will constitute a veritable merry-go-round that may provide a pleasant diversion, but that will absolutely fail to achieve a useful or durable framework for continuing exchanges or significant scholarship about its significance for religion. With this end in view, permit me to offer some distinctions -- which may indeed appear arbitrary. My point is that if we will to make important distinctions, and are tenacious in holding to them, our efforts will be significantly repaid.

"Modern," "modernism," "modernity" and related terms taken alone or qualified or compounded face us every day in the popular media as well as in more specialized journals and technically informed exchanges. I think that part of their ubiquity is due to the shifting sets of meaning the terms carry. That is, of course, a part of their usefulness; they permit us to communicate in ways that seem to be effective without ever requiring us to specify exactly what we mean. Citing the Mad Hatter as authority, let me suggest certain useful distinctions among and between the terms.

First, "modern" is a correlative term and indicates that which is new as opposed to that which is ancient, that which is innovative as opposed to that which is traditional. To say this implies several different things. For one, it implies that what is judged modern at this point in time and place in culture will not necessarily be thought of as that in the future or in some other context. Therefore, "modern" means relative to other times and places whether specified or not; it involves implicitly a comparison between times.

As a consequence, it follows that what is now thought to be "modern" will not always appear in that light. Thus, "modern architecture" of the mid-twentieth century now has a distinctly dated look as, I suppose, nineteenth century symphonic music seemed modern to those brought up on the baroque. Endless examples spring to mind that would make this point vividly. Especially as scholars of long-term cultural patterns we understand as religion, we must not fail to put in perspective changing perceptions of what is new, what is dated.

Additionally, it also follows that what may appear in one setting as "modern" may in another framework seem much more rooted in a cultural tradition. And this may suggest that what appears as ancient or settled was once itself, at one point at least, experienced as new.

I take it that "modernism" is an explicit and self-conscious commitment to the modern in intellectual and cultural matters (or at least support of the claims of the new as against its critics and detractors), even as "modernization" is a programmatic commitment to remake the political and economic orders in support of the new. Thus we are more likely to speak of "modernism" in nineteenth-century Roman Catholicism or in twentieth-century American Protestantism, or even among the Hindus, than we are of the "modernization" of a religious tradition. At the same time, we refer to the "modernization" of the factory or of a tax structure, but not, with respect to those matters, of "modernism" -- unless we are talking about factory architecture in the one case or art objects as shelters under the IRS code in the other.

So for our purposes "modernism" implies a commitment to the modern in religion -- and often is linked to comparable commitments in other fields. This introduces the thought that modernisms may not be divisible -- attitudes towards art, music, religion, productive labour, and so forth may hang together and form a powerful set of interactive commitments. Here we see the shadow of an argument that secularization may be relentlessly supplanting the old with the new, and that in the course of the process it is making claims upon those who accept it that in terms of their characteristics seem to be "religious" -- that is, ultimate and unqualified.

At this point, our term "modernity" enters. For it implies a statement of commitment to the new as opposed to the old. Note that we moved from remarking upon the modern as a given in contemporary life to identifying commitment to it as social modernization or cultural modernism; now with "modernity" an additional move is made to reify this consciousness of cultural change so that it seems to have a content roughly equivalent to that similarly reified threat, "secularity." As scholars I think we must resist this attribution of substantiality to attitudes and activities. There may indeed be a congruence between the many aspects of a modern culture which, to those who resist them, may make them seem the expression of a powerful entity in its own right. But this reification only forecloses what ought to be a subject for analysis; it serves to confuse our perception, and gives over the one power we exercise as scholars, namely consistent and precise use of language. My plea is that we use language with extreme care at this point. It is not helpful to use the term "modernity" as if it represented a spiritual medium in contemporary life. It is much more useful to have it as a means of recognizing that cultural change is pervasive -- or experienced as that, though to greater or lesser degrees in various contemporary societies.

One of the consequences of reifying modernity in the manner suggested is that by definition it has settled the issue which scholars must insist remain under discussion. So to conceive of modernity as a spiritual medium that envelopes and interconnects all particular instances of commitment to modernization is to posit a preeminently religious phenomenon. As a consequence, modernity itself is presumed to be a rival to traditional or "authentic" religion. One implication is that a dichotomous or bivalent view of religion in the world is necessarily created. X is either for modernity and thus against traditional religious commitments or for traditional religion -- and thus antipathetic towards modernity in any and all forms. I intend to develop the point that this very dichotomous or bivalent view, at least in an intense version, is a special characteristic of periods of cultural change generally, and of the cultural change we label modernity in particular. At the same time I want to argue that, under conditions of modernity, one (of many) responses is the attempt to reaffirm traditional cultural forms as unchanging -- albeit in particular versions and with new vigour.

If we take modernity in a more descriptive sense, then there is little doubt that the decisive commitment to modernization socially and to modernism culturally is to be observed most fully developed over time as a coherent process on the North American continent. It might be argued that currently Japan, shall we say, or in the last decades of the eighteenth century, revolutionary France, represent more thorough-going examples of commitment to the "modern." It certainly may be that for brief periods other societies have manifested more intense commitment to change. But over a time, at least to date, North American society has set about, more thoroughly than anywhere else, to overcome traditional ways and to replace them with new ones. In sum, I am arguing that Canada and the United States are, if we stretch our language a bit, laboratories in which we may observe the modern. Here we might look for the kinds of cultural changes attendant upon modernization of society that would enable us to identify what seems to happen to religion under the condition of relentless change.

If we can thus distinguish the fact of cultural change from a postulated spiritualized (and thus reified) modernity as itself the controlling religious commitment, we will be in the position to review much more open-mindedly what seems to have happened to religion under the conditions of prolonged change -- at least in these laboratories. If the postulate of a reified modernity drops out of the picture, the actual changes we can observe seem to be remarkably heterogeneous, that is, the changes are by no means of one type, nor do they run in one direction only.

At this point, I think it is important to focus for a moment on the relationship between cultural change and modernism. Put exactly, the latter is a special case of the former. Cultural change has been a given in human societies throughout historic time. There have been periods of more and less intensive cultural change -- but there certainly is not any society we know anything about that has been altogether free of it. Obviously our records for ancient societies do not permit refined distinctions, but our access to more recent historical ones allows us to offer some generalizations. For one thing it is possible to identify characteristic religious responses to periods of intensive cultural change. One kind of change is the development of a dichotomous view of the world -- civilized versus heretics, etc; the sets of categories have been numerous but their essential bifurcation of the world is well known. Another has been "enhancement" of orthodoxy, orthopraxy, or tradition. This is the case in terms of both ancient and recent examples of interaction between cultures and within a culture. A third is the frequent millenarian or apocalyptic response. This occurs when the change is experienced as so threatening and intense that it is believed that the "big change" will necessarily occur.

Cast in this framework we should see our modern era as a special case of social and cultural change. Among other things it is, if you will, self-conscious about social and cultural change. Some characteristic attitudes towards religion may indeed mark it, but these tend to be special cases of more general attitudes to change and not wholly different species. For example, with respect to our era, "modernization" includes a systematic commitment to rationality, which is to say the conviction that logically consistent and universalizable principles ought to be the basis for change. Again, "modernism" tends to undervalue the role of symbols and the subconscious. A third and related attitude is that human life is highly plastic or malleable. Now this set - and it is not enumerated as a full set by any means -- is surely a special case of social and cultural change, but it is a special case of what is a historic, perhaps even universal, phenomenon. We simply do not have our distinctions straight if we think it is unique or sui generis. My somewhat ironic comment is that we are dealing with mirror images. Hostility to the modern, on the part of religious traditions, is simply a negative response to change, as modernism is an uncritical acceptance of it. An explicit and positive attitude towards social and cultural change is no more inherently derived from the change than a negative response is; both are typical attitudes towards change throughout history. Our task is to understand the modern, not to either embrace or excoriate it.

If we do not reify modernity as a spiritual entity, and if modernism is but a special and self-conscious case of positive cultural response to change, our proper subject ought to be how religion appears to differentiate under conditions of social and cultural change in the modern era. In this period which is conscious of the new, what are characteristic changes in religion?

We might begin with a useful distinction at this point between responses to modernity that represent a decisive reorientation of the whole tradition and those that represent the taking on of a coloration by, or the permeation of, a tradition so as to affect its tone and texture. Let me take the latter first to enable us to address explicit responses without "background static" as a result of failure to make this distinction.

Some of the responses are clearly due to the permeability of religious institutions by techniques and procedures which, once developed, are adopted throughout most sectors of the society. For example, religious organizations and bodies have adopted bureaucratic structures and business techniques. These are inevitably centralizing impulses, whether they have to do with means of communication (telephone calls not pastoral letters, personal visits not written reports), or with the liquidity of wealth. Do you suppose John Wesley could imagine the ability of a religious bureaucracy to raise funds and shift allocations throughout a global church? These kinds of change potentially strengthen the hands of such central figures as bishops and superintendents. But the same culture has also extended to the laymen both knowledge and the ability to challenge such a shifting of power to central authorities. So countervailing trends have set in, leading both to revitalization of local parishes and to extraecclesial religious organizations that, using the same techniques of the modern world, can raise and dispense funds, and exercise influence -- often against the authorities whose power is thus countered and blocked.

Other kinds of change have to do with the high degree of rationality required to function in a society of the scale and complexity of ours. Whereas the traditional religious bodies and ideas include myriad religiously oriented festivals and feasts, in modern society this does not work any longer. Thus we see withdrawal on the part of traditional religion from the public world, and an assertion of its possibly increased relevance to -- and control over -- private time and space.

Now, these I take to be examples of what we might term the "coloration" through which the new or modern context -- that is the contemporary period of intense social and cultural change -- influences in very basic ways all kinds of religious behaviours and beliefs. This is roughly comparable to ways that religions have always found it necessary to accommodate to the idioms, patterns of organization, and the symbolisms of their own times. Certainly in the contemporary world the degree of penetration by context may be different in some respects, but I think this is not a difference in kind. My basic point is to contrast this "coloration" or "permeability" of religious traditions by modern ways with much more explicit religious responses to the modern which strike me as strictly and properly identified as such.

I offer the following six-fold pattern or typology, wishing only to claim for it a certain utility in clarifying a great and generally confusing range of religious phenomena associated with modern social and cultural changes. It certainly does not pretend to the status of a model through which we might undertake to explain why the particular sets of characteristic responses have developed. It is not even clear that all relevant phenomena are equally well served by this sorting. I do think that the pattern does take account of the sense of integrity and compellingness within each of the religious responses, on the one hand, and, on the other, of the complex challenge -- of opportunity, fascination and threat -- posed by change, especially in the modern period. The patterns or categories form the following set:

1. The generation of new traditions, or the development of new insights into old traditions; these involve either embracing the new ostensibly as a means of correctly understanding the old or claiming that the old is correctly understood in new terms. An example of the first kind we find in the Oneida community and its founder John Humphrey Noyes. The modern common life of the community had its spiritual sources in early Christianity and claimed to be its completion. The

alternative pattern is illustrated in Christian Science whose founder, Mary Baker Eddy, believed that ancient truths were here first fully realized. These two fascinating movements represent an explicit kind of religious response to social and cultural change in the modern era.

2. Another kind of response we might think of as explicit accommodation to the new in terms that still maintain organic connections with the broader tradition. In this category we might place Protestant liberals, the Jewish Reformed tradition (which of course had its origins in accommodation to modern Europe at the time of Jewish Emancipation) and the Roman Catholic Americanists in late nineteenth century. All exemplify open acceptance of modern culture and did not believe it required them to compromise the basic religious tradition fatally.

3. A third pattern of response is the attempt at preservation of the continuing tradition, though self-consciously within the limits posed by the new framework. Here we might point to broadly Catholic constructions of the tradition which seem to have resources in terms of symbolic and ritual structures, as well as a sense that the specific tradition does indeed create a culture which has antiquity and resistance far beyond that apparent (yet) in the modern. The Mercersberg Movement in mid-nineteenth century America and the contemporary American Roman Catholic Church will suffice as examples of this strategy.

4. A fourth position is the strident reassertion of the old in a condensed, purified, or even reductionist form. Here we identify the strands of fundamentalism which have become apparent in most of the major religious traditions. Perhaps the American case makes clear, however, that the form in which the tradition is reasserted -- in this case propositions -- is itself given by the modern era. Fundamentalists are modern souls insisting on an ancient identity -- possibly to save themselves from themselves.

5. In a few instances we may recognize the generation of groups or cults which self-consciously celebrate the modern either without explicit reference to prior traditions or as independent of them. Here the content is given by modern culture -- although any who are knowledgeable about persistent sets of symbols, rituals, and myths will probably see refractions or even reincarnations of religious patterns which are as ancient as any human culture we have knowledge about. In this sense such groups or cults in our time are explicitly pagan and typically short-lived. Numerous examples come to mind from the era of counterculture; let me suggest one which has gained literary notoriety if not immortality thanks to Tom Wolfe -- Ken Kesey's Merry Pranksters as a

movement delineated and described in <u>The Electric Koolaid Acid Test</u>.

6. A sixth type or pattern is less readily discovered in our North American laboratories, and it is less purely a religious response to a social and cultural change in the sense that it directly serves other purposes as well in the society. This sets it off from the other kinds of responses. This type is the implicit, or in the extreme case, even explicit sponsorship and supervision by the state of cults celebrating its legitimacy in religious terms. Such phenomena are more typically present in societies where the form of government includes a well-developed and articulated state. Such is the case, for example, in the Japanese phenomenon of State Shinto. Perhaps a comparable phenomenon also exists in religious aspects in Nazi philosophy and policy. The strong tradition especially in the United States of divided governmental powers and the ostensible separation of church and state helps to explain its relative absence in the North American setting. It is, however, a potentially interesting framework within which civil religious phenomena might be explored to advantage. The civil cultic phenomena would be, in this framework, at least in part a response to social and cultural changes in the modern world that we are designating as modernity.

This six-fold pattern is, I am fully aware, an arbitrary dividing of a spectrum more than a circle, for the extremes don't meet. But the chief point is the great variety in the religious responses to intense social and cultural change, indeed dare we say, when the phenomenon of coloration is taken into account, that no religious expression is unaffected by the modern setting. It serves our purposes if it helps to make clear that the explicit relationships between religion and modern culture are not single or of one kind only. They vary greatly. They are so plural that respective religious movements responding to social and cultural change in modernity may, in fact, be directly opposed to each other and certainly are often in high tension with each other.

At one extreme, cultural changes identified as modernity can be embraced so whole-heartedly that new or distinctive religious cults celebrate modernity -- though aspects of the content may be ancient. At the other extreme, rejection of the modern leads to emergence of religious groups that may make formal claims to continuity with tradition, but in substance they in fact represent accommodation to, if not an embrace of, the modern and the institutionalization of that response.

Thus I conclude that modern times or the modern era has proven to effect religion heterogeneously. Religious responses to modernity range so broadly as to involve strong and strident reassertions of traditions, frequently on a reduced basis, as well as an outright and uncritical embrace of cultural change. Modernity should thus be seen as identifying a period of intense social and hence cultural change. In this it is not unique, and its influence scarcely unanticipated. Only in the sense of "permeation" or "coloration" does it seem helpful to identify a peculiar configuration as determined by "modernization" in its impact upon cultural practices generally and religious ones in particular. But this does not point to the conclusion that "modernity" is to be seen as itself a spiritual medium, that is to say, a religion.

There is, however, one additional aspect of the relation between modernity and religion that requires brief notice. One by-product of modernity, and perhaps also an engine of the changes that constitute modernity, is development of what some have called the "knowledge industry." That certainly prominently includes universities as institutions specializing in analysis of society and culture, past, present, and future. In the development of modern universities an increasingly explicit place has been given to the study of religion, that is to say, recognition that aspects of human social and cultural life presuppose and point to fundamental premises, ultimate questions, or boundary situations. In part this recognition comes through the volume and variety of attention to gods and goblins, redemption and despair in traditional departments like history, English, sociology, or anthropology. Increasingly it is also due to the emergence of departmental programs in the study of religion. These are not directed, it should be noted, to the study of Christianity, or Judaism, or Buddhism, or Islam -- but to religion. This is new. In one sense, of course, it is a part of the permeability of traditional institutions by modern attitudes and practices. But it also reminds us that cultures vary and religious postures are multiple. This is a very different perspective on religion than that taken from within a tradition itself. I would argue in a somewhat ironic fashion that this may be the single most significant development associated with modernity that affects religion in new ways in our time. Those of us whose professional lives are so defined should be the first to recognize this interface between modernity and religion. It is possibly the one decisively new factor in the situation we are working to understand.

Note: This kind of typology bears some relationship to H.R. Niebuhr's in Christ and Culture (N.Y.: Harper, 1951), except in that case his categories were tightly developed as a set of logical

relationships between the terms. That is much less a characteristic of this venture. It is also quite different from the
analysis offered by Linda Pritchards of the Second Great Awaken-
ing (see "Religious Change in Nineteenth Century America," in C.
Glock and R. Bellah, eds., The New Religious Consciousness,
Berkeley: University of California Press, 1976).

MODERN RELIGION AS FOLK RELIGION
Robert S. Ellwood, Jr.

I

My purpose is to present some summaries and perspectives which I hope may be of use in the ongoing debate over secularization and the future of religion. It seems to me that this debate has reached a kind of stasis because of definitional ambiguities and a failure to examine hidden assumptions on all sides which need to be cleared away before real headway can be made in understanding what is actually happening to religion in the modern world.

For believers in secularization, the decline of religion in recent times is an obvious fact, the sort of thing that "everyone knows," and indeed they often seem to respond to their critics with a hint of irritation that supposedly intelligent people should refuse obstinately to accept such a patent reality, as though talking to a flat-earther. On the other side, critics point to their own obstinate facts about the persistence and even prosperity of religion in the modern world, its amoeba-like ability to reshape and multiply itself to fill countless new niches in social ecology, and query whether a theory which requires so many qualifications and superimposed epicycles to make it fit the facts may not be a sociological equivalent of Ptolemaic astronomy.

Nonetheless secularization as an idea persists, and in fact is accepted in some form by almost all important sociologists and historians of religion. This is no doubt first of all because, as Durkheim implied at the very end of The Elementary Forms of the Religious Life, [1] and as Bryan Wilson has more recently observed, [2] secularization is indicated by the very nature of the sociological enterprise itself. For if, as the latter must assume, religion can be interpreted, in part or in whole, by sociological analysis, then (that) religion is dethroned as absolute monarch and subjected to a higher law. In Durkheimian language, if the real though unacknowledged object of religion is society itself, then religious knowledge can be replaced by sociological knowledge, and must be when the latter arrives on the scene. The sociologist by the very act of sociologizing also secularizes, and insofar as his work has any impact on the attitudes of society as a whole its secularization is furthered.

The fathers of sociology, from Comte, Durkheim, and Weber on down, assumed in effect Peter Berger's definition of secularization as "the process by which sectors of society and culture are removed from the domination of religious institutions and symbols," together with its subjective corollary, the "secularization of consciousness."[3] They then proceed to explain how and why this removal has come to pass, and to deal with questions of to what extent religion has a future. Here differences have ensued.

The role of religion in society has been studied basically from two sociological perspectives. One, stemming from Emile Durkheim, has emphasized its origin in society itself and its role in giving cohesion to society, in providing the myths, rituals, values, and sense of identity as a community that bind a community together on the level of symbol and feeling and induce members to make pro-community choices. The other, based on the work of Max Weber, stresses what may be called the cognitive and operational aspects of religion: its way of providing knowledge of the supernatural and of managing human response to it or manipulation of it. For Weber this knowledge and power was primarily transmitted to and through individuals -- charismatic persons, magicians, and priests -- rather than residing in a Durkheimian social effervescence, though of course its social impact, as well as its indirect origin in societal problems and needs, is very great, and indeed the exploration of the interrelationship was Weber's abiding concern.

These two approaches are not necessarily inconsistent, and most subsequent work in the sociology of religion has drawn from both. But each creates a different emphasis in the understanding of religion with immense bearing on the problem of secularization. We shall examine them each in turn, beginning with the Durkheimian.

If religion resides in the cohesion of society, its health depends on the extent to which society coheres, and likewise the extent to which religious symbols and acts reinforce this cohesion without people being aware that, rather than transcendent religious realities, it is society that is the true object of religious feeling. An extreme Durkheimian can argue that if society is the true focus of religion, then there will be religion so long as there is society, since all societies by definition have some kind of unifying symbol and structure. This proposition has led to some rather quixotic theories suggesting that seemingly secular media of social bonding, from Maoism in China before the reaction against the Great Cultural Revolution to the spirit of American pragmatism, are "really" religious despite the lack of a supernatural referent.

While this approach obviously illumines important functional continuities, it makes the definition of religion so elastic as to render the word less useful than it ought to be. In light of religion's historic meanings concerned with public and private structures of thought and behaviour expressing awareness of supernatural reality, one would expect to see in something properly called religion that awareness conveyed simultaneously through, say, Joachim Wach's three forms of religious expression: the theoretical, practical, and sociological.[4] In this vein Peter Berger has criticized Thomas Luckmann's interesting argument in The Invisible Religion,[5] that religion is any universe of meaning human beings create to manifest their capacity to transcend biological nature. In effect, then, any social phenomenon becomes at least potentially religious. But Berger argues, when modern science, for instance, becomes a form of religion, as it may under Luckmann's definition, the utility of the word is weakened. Berger prefers to limit religion to the positing of a sacred cosmos, an objective moral/spiritual order legitimated by supernatural reality, by the sacred in something like Rudolf Otto's or Mircea Eliade's sense.[6] Under this definition we can take note of the countless permutations the sacred, in its dialectic with the profane, is able to take, but at the same time the possibility of true secularization, the disappearance of the sacred altogether, cannot be ruled out.

Peter Berger is Durkheimian insofar as he assumes as his base point the social construction of a sacred reality which unifies cosmos, society, and the individual into a seamless whole. He likewise perceives a progressive disruption of this primordial whole in history. This disruption has roots as far back as the Old Testament and the Reformation, and it involves a "disenchantment of the World," in which demarcations are made between the sacred and the secular, with the former more and more pushed to some transcendent point beyond the confines of this world altogether, or restricted to "specialized" institutions such as the Christian church.

This is, clearly, a social process of secularization, even though as Berger tried to show in A Rumor of Angels the experiential sources of religion have not necessarily dried up.[7] But they have become highly personal, privatized, and at best express themselves only in highly relativistic religious forms within a pluralistic situation; in a disenchanted world the transcendent must be found in whatever fragmented bits and pieces it can, and only the most obdurate will to believe can sustain more than a functionally relativistic belief in the truth of each. The "sacred canopy" of old is shattered.[8]

An important aspect of the Durkheimian tradition is the Civil Religion discussion, associated with Will Herberg and Robert Bellah. Despite the obviously fragmented pluralism of religion in the United States, these writers contend, there has also been in that country a common if attenuated religious expression centred on such doctrines as belief in a divine providence guiding the destiny of the nation, together with ceremonies and symbols of the state as a community with sacred meaning. These workings have counterbalanced the rampage of pluralism and saved something of the Durkheimian function. However one evaluates it, though, civil religion has apparently not proved of adequate mettle to withstand the onslaughts of secularization. Herberg regarded it as little more than a pious facade, of little weight compared to the testimony of the traditional faiths.[9] Bellah, who takes its significance as an expression of shared values even in a pluralistic situation more seriously, has acknowledged that in recent decades it has become a "broken and empty shell."[10] If values unite Americans, they are now wholly secular, pragmatic ones, without even such a vestigial sacred canopy legitimating them as civil religion. In true Durkheimian fashion, when the social nature of the sacred is discovered, its days are numbered, and sociological knowledge has replaced religious truth.

The question of the future of religion is, then, in Durkheimian terms, one of whether religion can persist when fragmented into bits strewn through a society still reasonably homogeneous in all respects but religion. For despite much talk of general fragmentation, it is clear that a modern nation like the United States is still largely unified in most important areas but religion, and indeed owing to the effects of mass media and rapid transportation may be becoming more so. The government is not about to collapse, a complex and well-meshed economic system sends standard brands out to the remotest hamlet, people laugh and weep at the same TV series in Maine and California, and all in all the educational system is turning out more and more identical products across the land so far as their secular skills and attitudes are concerned.

Only religion, despite its sometime attempts to market comparable standard brands and to employ the same mass media, seems incapable of attaining a similar unity. It does not really unite supposedly one-religion countries like Spain or Sweden any more, and much less, apart from the remnants of civil religion, a country like the U.S. Otherwise identical engineers may be agnostics or fundamentalists; clean-cut Catholics and Quakers may enjoy the same Disneyland rides or TV shows side by side. Perhaps it doesn't matter; on the other hand it doesn't jell.

It may be, as Peter Berger tells us, "increasingly difficult to maintain the religious traditions as unchanging verity"[11] in this situation. Religious groups can only shore up their own particular subworld and hope that, so far as their universal validity is concerned, the civil religion golden rule of "No Offence" is kept and no one will be so uncivil as to point out that, so far as any reasonable claim to universal validity is concerned, with so many emperors trying to share the imperial vestments each individual one is at best wearing only a few tatters.

Nonetheless, it is obvious that some powerful force, some slow inertia or nuclear bonding, is keeping religious consciousness awake and religious groups alive despite what in terms of Durkheimian sociology ought to look like a pretty desperate situation. Their social-cohesion role dissipating (save as it still serves class or ethnic needs), their claims to pluralism, their inability to move toward the same sort of homogenization as the rest of American culture painfully obvious -- what sort of hope can religious groups in the U.S. have? Yet they persist and even flourish. We shall return to this paradox.

II

First, however, let us turn to the Weberian tradition. Here, if religion is the knowledge and operation of supernatural realities, then its health depends on the extent to which this knowledge is credible and the institutions devoted to its transmission accepted as legitimate, and able to adapt themselves to changing conditions.

Some Weberians paint a picture somewhat rosier for religion than is common in the contemporary Durkheimian camp with its elegies for a sacred canopy. Talcott Parsons, for example, has contended that religion has in fact adapted itself with some success. He acknowledges that when societies were simple, elements we might call religious and others we might not were fused together in a single web of meaning like Berger's sacred canopy. As societies grew more complex, "differentia-tion" set in, with religious and secular institutions assuming different functions. Indeed religious and worldly components of the individual psyche came to be differentiated. But this process, which some might call secularization, does not necessarily mean that religion is becoming less significant. In a world of specialists, religious specialists may be as credible as any other. Indeed, the fact that religion is increasingly individualized, and in a pluralistic world a matter of individual choice, might well serve to make it more important to an individual as such than when it was a more or less automatic part of tribal life. Further, religion's moral influence on seemingly secular institutions such as business and politics in a nation with a religious heritage may be indirect, but cannot be discounted. [12]

Andrew Greeley, combining both Durkheimian and Weberian approaches, comes to a similar cautiously optimistic view. There will always be religion, he asserts, since society required it on Durkheimian grounds. While perhaps a society theoretically could cohere on non-religious values, no empirical evidence exists for this happening satisfactorily. But Greeley also argues for Parson's differentiation theory and Berger's pluralism, affirming that the Durkheimian role can be played by differentiated, pluralistic religion in a complex society. Under modern conditions, when fragmentation is a given of human experience, it does not automatically disqualify religion in the eyes of most; Greeley responds to Berger's ruminations on this matter by pointing to the fact that it is precisely in the countries where religion is most pluralistic or even polarized, such as Holland, Ireland, and the United States, that it is apparently most healthy. In the modern world, competition among religions is expected, and far from weakening faith seems to keep it alive and alert. [13]

Another sociologist who is sceptical of secularization hypotheses, but who is somewhat hard to place theoretically, is David Martin. His basic theory of religion seems to be Weberian in that it is cognitive, having to do with an "orientation towards the world" that includes a "transcendent vision," [14] which has an operative role parallel to that of science. But of his own theory of secularization, he says "Durkheim provided the frame." [15]

Fundamentally, though, Martin has conducted a campaign of elegant rearguard fencing against proponents of general secularization theories. He is not so unwise as to say there is nothing to secularization at all. In an essay on secularization and the arts, he discusses the common observation that the style and content of music and the visual arts have become progressively more secular since the Middle Ages. But he contends that this is not necessarily a barometer of society generally, but its instances can all be given special explanations. The change and decay which all around he sees in this particular field is, he holds in good High Tory fashion, to be blamed on the influence of French culture, for reasons we will note shortly.

So far as secularization as a "unified syndrome of characteristics subject to an irreversible master-trend" is concerned, it is an illusion. He makes the usual arguments that the data are inconsistent and difficult to interpret, that even where religious participation can be shown to be declining, as in his own England, a "subterranean theology" of religious-type attitudes persists, and that secularizing sociologists are blinded to these things by their own arbitrary definitions and reductionistic assumptions about religion. [16]

Nonetheless, the man who once said that the word secularization "should be erased from the sociological dictionary" [17] later wrote a book called A General Theory of Secularization. Here David Martin argues for a short-term, "highly empirical" use of the concept. Again the French Revolution and its ilk are blamed for what reality there may be to secularizing trends. The latter stem from a vicious circle set in motion when religion and a substantial part of the population are polarized against each other, as was the church and its largely reactionary supporters against the working class and liberal opinion in France during the revolutionary era, a gulf through, gulf which, as is well known, long remained a deep cleavage in French society. This disaster is apt to occur when society and religion are first posited in "monopolistic" terms as was Catholicism in France especially after the revocation of the Edict of Nantes; in countries like Holland and the U.S., where two or more faiths have long shared spiritual sway, the French experience is not likely to recur. [18] However oversimplified this interpretation of religious history (and of course I have oversimplified Martin's book-length presentation of it), its kernel of truth serves to reinforce Greeley's contention that secularization is spotty and often illusory, and that religious pluralism, far from being the terminal symptom of secularization in the modern world, may actually be its antidote.

Martin's cautious and critical use of the secularization concept is continued in his Dilemmas of Contemporary Religion, [19] in which, looking to the short-term future of Western religion, he anticipates a weakening of the central core of Euro-American cultural life through liberal pluralism and critical scepticism, but expects this decay will be met at the periphery by ethnic and religious resistance.

One sociologist who has few doubts about the reality of the secularization process is another British scholar, Brian Wilson.[20] As befits the Weberian tradition, Wilson is inclined to give more significance to changes in the cognitive than in the social role of religion. Here he sees little ground for hope that religion, in anything like its traditional form, will rise again. The real change the world is undergoing is not in formal religious belief or practice, but in regard for the supernatural, in everyday belief in miracles, witches, and the like. On this front the real underpinnings of mass religiosity are being cut away. Those "secular" theologians and their sociological allies who attempt to salvage a religion without the old-fashioned supernatural are too sophisticated by half and of little relevance to the true situation.

For Wilson, the sort of theory that says a modern man is "really" religious because he washes his car religiously every Sunday morning or his ultimate concern is loving his wife or mistress, or that sees the modern miracle-free church as more than the residue of a dying heritage, is simply engaging in definitional sleight-of-hand. Religion, if it means anything, must mean a downright belief that the supernatural is real and impinges readily and often on ordinary human life. This belief, and behaviour associated with it, has been steadily dissipated by science and the march of modernity, even in people who think of themselves as religious. Therefore religion has declined and secularization advanced.

Put this way, I suppose even the most ardent antisecularization theorist, after much hemming and hawing, would have to agree, although anyone who had been around evangelical and charismatic circles can affirm that the supernatural with signs following is still a good way from total decline in even the supposedly most advanced societies.

The inevitability of the process, however, is advocated by Wilson in his response to a rambling, learned article by Daniel Bell. The latter argued eloquently, if not with particular originality, that religion does not die but changes.[21] Like others, he granted that there is a process of secularization as religion retreats from various areas of public life, but insisted it is only pulling back to its invulnerable redoubt in the private sphere. Religion, Bell insisted, can operate in the cultural and personal lives of persons without being socially functional or affected by changes in social structure. This is ultimately because it deals with perennial human questions and concerns for meaning which persist regardless of social change.

Wilson answered that religious attitudes do, in fact, follow changes in society, though perhaps with a time-lag. Any view that culture and belief for the average person can be hermetically sealed off from what is going on in the society of which he or she is a part is hopelessly naive or elitist. Belief in hell, for example, has notably declined with the modern rise in living standards, as this world has become for most far less of a vale of tears than formerly. In the same way, private religion cannot forever survive a loss of public function or social reason for its worldview. The meaning questions may, of course, continue to be asked, but this does not mean they need to be put or answered in religious terms, which as we have seen would mean for Wilson supernatural terms. [22]

Despite such objections as these, others too have seen a future for religion in the personal arena. Huston Smith has forcefully argued that the retreat of an institution from certain public roles to more private ones is not necessarily an unstoppable process which will lead to the institution's demise in the end. He points to the parallel example of the family, which also no longer plays as public a role as it once did, or is generally as "extended" as it once was, but which shows no evident sign of disappearing. Rather, despite all the strains on the residual nuclear, personal-life family, people continue to marry and remarry, and to move out of the family as autonomous individuals into the workaday world, then at the end of the workday withdraw back to it as the venue of personal, private life.

Family and personal life, on the one hand, and public and occupational life, on the other, are today separable and detached in a way unimaginable even a hundred years ago, when the family farm, the family business, the home above the shop, and family ties helping one get ahead, whether prince or commoner, were the way of the world; now all these concepts are pale shadows of their former power: husband and wife are each more likely to be autonomous individuals in the business or professional world, while whether one happens to live in a family in one's off-hours or not means very little out there.

Yet for all that, the family lives on in the personal sphere. Can there be a message here, Smith implies, for the future of religion? Perhaps secularization, like defamilization, can proceed only so far in the world as we know it. [23]

The obvious difference, however, is that the family has a base in biological and nurturing imperatives which most people, despite proposed alternatives, seem to find compelling. The sociobiologists notwith-

standing, religion apparently has no imperative on quite the same level
as that which sets men and women in families: it is either more personal
or more social.

III

Let us sum up the discussion so far. Virtually all students of
secularization would agree that, so far as its visible moral and institutional impact is concerned, religion has progressively withdrawn from
several major areas of human life in recent centuries, though much
difference obtains on whether this is a general or special phenomenon
and whether it is reversible. Richard K. Fenn has offered a detailed
model for this process, indicating the five major stages by which
religion moves from being an undifferentiated cement of society as a
whole to the increasingly "privatized" faith of many moderns. They are:

1. Separation of distinct religious institutions.

2. Demand for clarification of the boundaries between religious
and secular issues.

3. Development of generalized beliefs and values that transcend
the potential conflict between the larger society and its component
parts. (This stage attempts to cover over the wound left by the separation of religion from the rest of society; it produces ideology and also
civil religion.)

4. Minority and idiosyncratic definitions of the situation. (This
step includes the attempts of "withdrawal" sects and cults to return to
the undifferentiated situation for themselves at the cost of antagonism
toward the "mainstream" settlement.)

5. The separation of the individual from corporate life. (This
means the ultimate privatization of spiritual life as ideology and
sectarianism finally fail to compensate for the loss of undifferentiated
faith.)[24]

We shall now see how a process like this can be applied to the
secularization of modern life in recent centuries. (Although most
commentators rightly recognize that the process can be traced back to
the dawn of civilization and before, we shall like most use the high
Middle Ages as a starting point for the modern rise of secularization.)
Five areas can be briefly enumerated. (The list is my own, but similar
lists have been suggested by many writers.)

1. Economic. To speak only of Europe, the power which the Christian church held in the economic life of the Middle Ages through its

role as landowner and political force, and through such moral influences as its ban on usury, has greatly diminished. Capitalism, as it replaced the feudal order so congenial to ecclesiastical authority, enjoyed no institutional investment from religion. One can, of course, rightly argue with Weber, Parsons, and others that capitalism was fired in no small part by the new "inner asceticism" of the Protestant outlook, and that its values still have a real though unspoken role in modern economic institutions. But the very fact that these values have become largely unspoken in religious terms, and have no clear tie to visible religion, contrasts markedly with the feudal situation and would seem to many an unmistakable sign of long-term secularization abetted by the Reformation's "disenchantment" of the medieval world. For the whole process is a clear example of Fenn's demand for demarcation between the sacred and secular, the economic order being declared secular (save as, of course, godly men may be working in it) as the medieval world passed into the modern, even though the church remained a power in its own separate sphere.

2. _Politics._ The intimate though often uneasy medieval alliance of church and state has clearly given way to separation for all practical purposes. Even in those nations which still retain a nominal state church, its influence on day-to-day policy-making is minimal, and not even predictable when issues of great moral or institutional interest to it are at stake. As in the economic arena, a dwindling residual influence may remain in the "values" of the state, as articulated by civil religion and the pieties of politicians. In terms of Fenn's steps, countries such as England and France which once had robust state religions have now virtually reached his fourth stage; they have seen the boundaries of religion "clarified" at the cost of severe national polarization, have passed through enthusiasms for surrogate national ideologies, and now Anglicanism and French Catholicism are acquiring sectarian characteristics in their homelands.

3. _Education._ In a comparable way, education has moved from being, if not quite the ecclesiastical monopoly sometimes supposed, at least subject to heavy religious weight on all sensitive matters to generally secular control and content in Europe and America. The rise of classical and scientific studies at the Renaissance, the establishment of public schools, and the end of mandatory conformity to Anglicanism in English universities in the last century were landmarks in this trend. Although some European school systems retain token religious instruction, most education is now non-religious in schools and

universities operated by the State, as most are; religious education must be obtained voluntarily in religious institutions. For many people, both those who applaud and those who fear secularization, nothing symbolizes and actualizes more effectively than this the peripheral character of religion after centuries of secularization. For nowhere has the boundary of religion been more carefully drawn, surrogate ideologies more persuasively preached, religion pushed into sectarian stances, and indeed the last stage of the privatization of religion more nearly approached than in the field of education.

4. <u>Art and Literature</u>. Perhaps no process of secularization is more dramatic or, one might add, more puzzling and deeply ominous for religion than the decline of the sacred in art and letters. Puzzling because what it really means is that over the centuries religion has held less and less interest for the most intelligent and creative members of society, and for this there is no easy explanation except those arguments that are really circular; ominous because one wonders with what sort of vigour religion can survive without the support of such persons. The pattern is clear: several centuries ago the bulk of great music, sculpture, painting, and writing was permeated with religious themes; today, while there is still plenty of third-rate religious art, that which could be called original and distinguished is miniscule. In Europe decline of the sacred in art has been irregular; although the nineteenth century brought forth little that was not highly derivative (though some of it of considerable technical skill) in religious music, painting, and architecture, with its various "revivals" of gothic and so forth, in letters it still gave us fresh religious visions as rich as those of Gerard Manley Hopkins and Dostoevsky. But in the twentieth century the harvest has been skimpier yet. With the exception of a few self-conscious traditionalists like T.S. Eliot, the most powerful spiritual visions in the arts have been more from persons who seem precursors of an age of privatized faith than from those who are church-oriented; in this respect one could start with Blake and Beethoven, and mention such twentieth century persons of uncovenanted grace as Scriabin, Camus, and Le Corbusier.

5. Finally, we come to the <u>decline of religious institutions</u> which have attempted to parallel the other major institutions of society, that is, the great national denominations which in the nineteenth and twentieth centuries established public identities, bureaucracies, and local branches comparable to those of the state, a great corporation, or a school system. Much evidence lately has suggested that this pattern is

slowly breaking down. Tension and even schism between local congregations and the national organizations are on the increase, and cross-
denominational alternative structures, both local and national, often
compete successfully with the denominations, suggesting movement into
Fenn's step of minority and idiosyncratic definitions. The growing
frequency of church-switching tells us that denominational loyalty is
fading as an important value for many people. William R. Swatos has
suggested that religion is reverting to its natural base, localism, as
it seeks to preserve its identity against adverse trends in the general
culture, trends against which denominations, precisely because they
parallel the structures of that same general culture with its national
and international political, corporate, and educational entities, are
ill-prepared to defend themselves. [25]

To this category may be added more subjective aspects of the
decline of conventional religion which could nonetheless be documented:
Bryan Wilson's decline of general belief in the supernatural, and the
decline of religion as an important influence on mainstream intellectual
life. Adequate discussion of the second point would require far more
attention than is possible in the present paper; here let us only allude
to the fact that while religion is still vital in many places, theology
seems to be taken much less seriously by intellectuals generally, and
indeed even by the churches, than it once was. Only a generation ago
theologians of the highest calibre like Karl Barth, Paul Tillich, or the
Niebuhrs were known to the thinking public, appeared on the cover of
Time magazine, and were regarded as at least significant thinkers by the
intellectual mainstream. Now, even though theologians of the merit of
Hans Küng or Jurgen Moltmann are at work, one is hard put to think of
any who has the public significance or intellectual impact of those
departed giants.

In sum, we have a situation in which religion as an institutional
force is losing power to affect political, economic, and educational
life, and religion as a cultural force is losing power to influence
music, literature, art, and intellectual life. Furthermore, what many
would see as the real foundation of religion, belief in the supernatural
and its intervention in human affairs, has faded until beyond doubt few
people in modernized society actively believe in it except for the
special cases required by their own orthodoxy, or unless validated by
science as parapsychological phenomena -- but any need for such validation gives the show away so far as the continuing authority of religion
is concerned.

Qualifications must be made, of course, but they do not seem to vitiate the overall picture. Jerry Falwell and his cohorts may be enjoying a probably brief hour of political influence in the U.S., but he is no medieval pope. Religion is clearly more powerful in politics, economics, and education in the Islamic world than elsewhere; I would argue this is because Islam, as a younger religion than Christianity, is now at a stage of development similar to that of the latter in the age of the Reformation.

But looked at in terms of centuries, the secularization pattern seems undeniable in Europe and America from the perspective of what has traditionally been the form and role of religion. Claims that religion can long survive in a chastened and personalized but nonetheless subjectively rich state may be true, but do little to reassure one about the prospects of a society as a whole, which religion once legitimated and in which it once flourished institutionally. We cannot forget that, while both Durkheim and Weber accepted the fact of secularization and regarded it as progress insofar as it brought a truer understanding of the reality of things, they were both fearful of its human consequences, if the transition from religious to scientific knowledge were not made skillfully. Durkheim feared social chaos without the bond of faith, and Weber the excessive bureaucratization of life as the social order was "rationalized" and charisma, along with the sacred, pushed to the periphery.

And yet ... and yet ... doubts nag at the bold assertion that religion is on the way out. It has too often been proclaimed on its deathbed before, and there are those statistics that seem to fly in the face of secularization. At least in the United States, according to polls, 40 percent of the population still participates weekly in a religious activity. People are converted, transformed, pray, give, and enjoy the fellowship of religious assemblies as though faith were still in its prime. They experience gifts of the Spirit and anticipate apocalypses while the "outside" world goes on in its secularizing way. According to recent Gallup polls, in 1978, 89 in 100 Americans prayed, 57 in 100 said religion was "very important" to them, and in 1976 1 in 3 reported having had a religious or mystical experience. [26]

True, survey evidence does show some trends not favourable to traditional religion. Robert Wuthnow cites evidence which shows that, at least in certain geographic areas, belief in a conventional theistic concept of God, and in life after death, has declined by as much as 20 percent between the 1940s or 1950s and the 1970s. In place of it, he sees an upsurge of beliefs of a "mystical" sort, which he interprets as claiming that "the very definition of reality itself is subject to human control," an interpretation that would make the rise of the mystical highly compatible with Fenn's last individualizing step in secularization. But Wuthnow is appropriately cautious in the use of such data, pointing to the complexity of "trends" in a country like America, but suggesting that diversity can only increase in the forseeable future. [27]

We have then a world of mysticism and salvation which shows no obvious sign of rapidly passing away. But that religious world is increasingly a separate world. It is sealed off by more and more profound barriers of language, interests, attitudes, and style of institutional life from the other world shaped by the patterns of thought and behaviour required by science, technology, secular education, and rational, post-religious politics and economics. Religion is, in a rather technical sense, a cultural world, but one without much creative interaction with the rest of "high" culture, though it has no small rapport, at least in America, with popular culture.

Even though, as we have seen, this separate religious world is experiencing the decay of those institutional structures, like the denomination or the Catholic church as a centralized, monolithic organization, that most parallel the rationalized, bureaucratic state, it would be a mistake to imply it is merely slipping into infinite fragmentation. The new religious world does have its structures and institutions. Denominations survive and their politics generate quite a bit of heat. Cross-denominational and local organizations thrive, along with structures of leadership which, whether in person or in the form of the TV shaman, contain large charismatic elements and structures of support which, more than most other economic arenas today, give considerable place to voluntary labour.

What is happening is that, precisely because of features like these, the structure and institutions of religion are becoming, in Weberian language, less rationalized and more charismatic, with such elements of rationalization as remain devoted not to the routinization of charisma but to its perpetuation as charismatic experience on the periphery of an increasingly rationalized world. Thus, in American religion, the most obviously successful organizations -- and these are in fact notoriously rationalized and bureaucratic on the operative level -- are those dedicated to evangelistic crusades and television preachers of great charismatic appeal.

This spiritual world, transmitted increasingly through the con-
tinual renewal of charisma rather than through routinized structures of
education and institution, has decreasing interaction with the "outside"
intellectual and cultural domain, whose values are no doubt rightly felt
to be unsympathetic as, for religion, thought and structure fall behind
faith and charisma. Religious institutions abide, but their value is
felt more as visible assurances of the mythos validating present
charisma and experience, as perpetuations of an Eliadean _illud tempus_
when faith was bright and fresh, than as major channels of the transmission of faith today. The transmission role today is dominated by books,
magazines, the electronic media, and the family and social milieu;
formal religious institutions have less and less control over the forms
in which faith is passed.

IV

What does all of this come to? To my mind, a highly appropriate
model could begin with Robert Redfield's concept of Great and Little
Tradition.[28] What we have, I think, is a religious Little Tradition
continuing unabated but cut off from a living Great Tradition.

First, let us review the essential features of Redfield's picture.
Restricting our discussion only to religion, the Great Tradition of a
society would mean the dominant religion as it is borne by its highly
educated elites, usually priests and monks (and usually only the cream
of these). In traditional societies, these elites can wield appreciable
political and economic power, and may well be closely associated with
the kings and aristocrats who patronize them and make their courts
centres of Great Tradition learning and culture. The elites' version of
the religion is highly literate, engaged in exegetical scriptural study
and works of philosophical theology; it is transmitted through education
of good quality.

The Great Tradition's institutional structures, needless to say,
are highly routinized, but can produce persons of rich though usually
conventional wisdom as well as placemen. Being aware of history because
of its closeness to the literary heritage and the centres of power, the
Great Tradition takes a long perspective and values institutional
stability. It tends in fact to emphasize the historical rather than the
cosmic aspects of the religious outlook, to prefer intellectual sophistication to unbridled feeling, to mistrust charismatic personalities,
and to value highly interaction with the society's "mainstream" cultural

and social life. It loves excellence in religious art and architecture, and those who patronize such excellence.

The Little Tradition is, in premodern societies, the same religion as it is understood and experienced by peasants who, being nonliterate, know things only as they are in the present or as secreted in myth. It has little concern with formal philosophy or history; it is oriented to cosmic rather than historical time, concentrates on worship and experience more than theory, and is basically transmitted through family and community and charismatic figures such as shamans, "holy men," and wise-women, as well as the local priestly representatives of the Great Tradition. In the villages, however, the last usually find they do well tacitly to accept as "implicit faith" the Little Tradition's understanding of things.

Thus for the Little Tradition, religion centres around seasonal festivals like Christmas, around family and community folkways, around things that are done like pilgrimage and rite, and non-rational experience like miracles and mysticism; all this rather than the books and culture of the Great Tradition. Little Tradition people are likely to feel, fundamentally, that they cannot really affect the course of society as a whole or the politics and policies and kings and courts — unless through provoking a miracle, that is, through a peasants' revolt, a revival, a crusade, rather than through rational means.

As Redfield emphasized, the Great and Little Traditions continually interact with each other. The Little Tradition receives its fundamental symbols from the Great, even though it may accommodate them to its ageless patterns, making them characteristically cosmic and atemporal and subjective rather than historical and philosophically rational. Saints become transcendent semi-divine powers rather than historical figures. The folk of the Little Tradition may perceive their coreligionists among the elites of the Great with a strange ambiguity, at once uncritically adulating them for their learning and hierarchical splendour and hating them for their relative wealth and prestige, and their presumed hypocrisy and self-importance.

For their part, the Great Tradition elite will look upon the Little Tradition with an ambivalent combination of admiration and bemused contempt. Sometimes, like the Slavophiles of Russia in the last century, they may pass through moods of holding that, for all its seeming naiveté, peasant faith is somehow really deeper and purer than their own. At other times, with Josephite passion, they may attempt, heavy-handedly, to reform it to their own standards. Sometimes rulers find it to their interest, or perhaps material to their own salvation, to patronize and take into their confidences an outstanding charismatic figure of impeccable Little Tradition background, a Gyogi in Nara Japan, a Rasputin, or a Billy Graham; the Great Tradition religious elites are more likely to remain aloof from such a one. On the other hand, there are persons who genuinely and effectively mediate between the two traditions, making the best of each accessible to the other, such as John Wesley and his Japanese counterpart, Ninomiya Sontoku.

As Redfield also points out, a Little Tradition can continue with a vigorous life of its own long after the Great Tradition which nurtured it has vanished, and perhaps been superseded by another. Thus the villages of Mayan Indians in the Yucatan which he studied, though superficially touched by the Catholic Great Tradition, still preserve Little Tradition usages grounded in the long-vanished Great Tradition of the Mayan Empire. "The shaman-priests of the villages," he reported, "carried on rituals and recited prayers that would have their full explanation only if we knew what were the ritual and the related body of thought at Chichen Itza or Coba." [29]

For while a Little Tradition no doubt benefits from interaction with a corresponding Great Tradition, and without it is bereft of important potential for sophistication and flexible, creative response to new situations, it has a capacity to survive indefinitely on its own level, continually renewing its charismatic wells and even surviving persecution.

It is this state that I see religion in Christian Europe and North America now entering. Like all great religions in civilized society, Christianity has long had both Great and Little Traditions. Its Great Tradition, as I trust secularization theory has demonstrated, has about run its course. But its Little Tradition, far from quickly following suit and meekly accepting the arrival of successor Great Traditions as evidence of its disconfirmation, shows every sign of preserving its own Little Tradition level of Christianity and perchance surviving as long as Mayan religion in the Yucatan.

The Little Tradition style of religion is what has variously been called Peasant Religion and Folk Religion, and within the context of modern society, Popular Religion. Peter W. Williams has recently made quite creative use of the category in a study of popular religion in America. As he correctly points out, the classic peasant or folk Little Tradition is only a "first form of religion we might call authentically popular,"[30] in contrast to elite religion or the religion of undifferentiated societies.

Popular religion today represents remnants of past Little Traditions, together with popular responses, both of rejection and of utilization, of the fruits of modernization and secularization. Bearing that in mind, I would nonetheless like to speak of modern religion as Folk Religion, as a Little Tradition style of religiosity, in order to emphasize the instructive parallels between today's religion and that of classic Little Tradition societies.

The differences between these two are obvious; strictly speaking modern religion is only metaphorically Folk Religion in the peasant sense. Most modern popular religionists are not genuinely illiterate, and have at their disposal not just the rude tools of a peasantry but all the fabulous devices of a high-tech age for travel, communication, and computing. But the fact remains that the Great Tradition meaning of literacy escapes them even as does any message contained in the medium. For modern popular as for Folk Religion, religious communication from scripture or testimony or preacher is essentially miraculous, experiential, and charismatic. The words of the Bible are miracle-producing charms, not historical texts whose exegesis requires persons of elite education; the revival or TV preacher is a shaman evoking an Other World of miracle and transformation, not a lecturer whose words require reasoned reflection.

V

This style of religion may seem superficially vulnerable to the vicissitudes of history and change; actually it is extraordinarily impervious to them, as in the case of the Maya. Let us survey some basic patterns of Little Tradition religion, and see how well suited they are to favour the survival of religion on this level for long periods. They are particularly well adapted, in fact, to assure the long-term survival of the religion in the absence of Great Tradition institutions.

1. Transmission through non-literary means. In traditional Folk Religion, this means the faith is passed on through folklore, community example, or oral and exemplary transmission from parent to child and from specialist (shaman, wise-woman, local priest) to disciple. In modern terms, it means transmission by media that are either non-written (preaching, radio, TV) or outside the literary mainstream, by traditions

and group attitudes essentially rooted in the local community, and by specialists who, though they may be seminary-trained, are basically oriented toward perpetuating locally grounded traditions rather than interaction with the intellectual mainstream. This means transmission through the electronic media, through books which though widely read are considered to inhabit a religious ghetto and never appear in mainstream book review columns or bestseller lists, through the immediacy of a locally experienced religion from which signs and wonders are not lacking, and through personalities legitimated more by charisma than education in divinity. All this works for survival, for it leaves faith untouched by the vicissitudes of bookish culture.

2. A local, personal, and experiential quality. This is contained in the previously-mentioned extra-literary style of transmission. This kind of transmission does not communicate ideas so much as trigger experiences. Transmitting words and gestures are "condensed symbols" which, in the familiar local cultural context, evoke paradigmatic experiences and images, from childhood, from earlier religious stirrings, from the conventional lore of the religion. The phenomenological sociologist Alfred Schutz, following William James, has discussed the various "sub-universes of meaning" which parallel ordinary, "working" reality: the worlds of dreams, fantasies, play, and religious reality. Moving from one to another involves a sort of "shock," he tells us, like falling asleep or waking up.[31] In the case of religious world, a trigger or condensed symbol, as well or better than rational exposition, can induce the sub-universe of the religion personally and experientially. This process too is crucial to Little Tradition survival. The Little Tradition survives because of its ability uncritically to accept the reality of its sub-universes in the face of potential disconfirmation by "working" reality, a disconfirmation which, as we shall see, increasingly weighs upon the Great Tradition. The fundamental reasons the Little Tradition possesses that ability are its local legitimation, where disconfirmation may not have much conscious strength; its regard for words as triggers rather than rational discourse; its willingness to balance the claims of rationality with those of personal life-story needs, and its counter attack in the form of "folk" criticism of the rationalism which is, for the Little Tradition, a value based in "foreign" (i.e., non-local and non-experiential) classes, needs, and traditions.[32]

3. Specialists who are, like the Mayan, basically shaman priests who perform sacerdotal functions in offering routinized prayers and

rites, but who derive their call from subjective experience. In the modern world, most popular evangelists, religious radio and TV personalities, ministers, and renowned saints fit this description; the story of their "call" and initiatory experiences is usually an important part of mythos, and it is continually renewed by an appeal based much more on charisma (which is properly endowed in such an experience) than overt routinization. This allows for perpetuation of leadership essentially outside the values of Great Tradition educational institutions, though these may be used formally; but leadership is really produced, then, by the same kinds of logically legitimated triggers that confirm and perpetuate the faith itself.

4. <u>Renewal of charisma in movements such as Cargo Cults, the Ghost Dance, Revivals, or the Charismatic Movement of the 1970s.</u> The Little Tradition can engender movements which seem to respond to new conditions in its own terms. We cannot here engage in a full-blown discussion of such movements as responses to modernity, a matter over which an immense amount of anthropological ink has been spilled. But we should note that while they may ultimately fail, such movements do "buy time" for conventional Little Tradition religion in hours of crisis, indeed in the face of the collapse of the corr onding Great Tradition before traumatic cultural shocks. They can preserve essentials of the Little Tradition, sometimes for as much as several generations, by appearing to meet the enemy with Folk Religion's own weapons: miracle, charisma, and tenacious belief. The combat itself reinvigorates the blood of the Little Tradition, usually bestows enough victories to give it fresh short-term validation, and suggests that if change is imperative it can change in its own way under the aegis of signs and visions and anointed leaders -- which also means it remains the same. The survival value of this capacity is obvious.

5. <u>Permanent, visible objects such as fetishes, holy pictures, scriptural books regarded as signs and triggers and as symbols of religious reality.</u> The stress on symbolic "hardware" also enables religion to elude confrontation with the Great Traditions' text and rational thought, and its vulnerable relationship with other major institutions. Instead it concentrates on that which, so long as the religion itself lasts, is self-validatingly holy.

In sum, the Little Tradition survives precisely because it avoids what the Great Tradition regards as the assurance of religious survival, reliance on the great texts, intellectual tradition, and institutional solidity. In this the Great Tradition's dependence on word, considered as vehicle for discourse rather than as talisman, is its most fundamental distinction of all. Most of all, the scholarly brahmin feels secure with the Vedas, and the learned bishop with the Bible, the Creeds, and the Church Fathers. This textual orientation need not be construed in any narrow, conservative sense; it is the charter of the theological liberal as much as the traditionalist, only the words (or their connotation) being different. Its spirit has been well put by David Tracy as he argues that the evolving life of a religion can be understood as ongoing dialogue with its great texts, not just as authoritarian submission to them.[33]

Yet the Great Tradition's word-orientation contains a fatal Achilles' Heel. It directly makes the religion's hierophany historical and so distanced in time and only a mediated experience. In Paul Ricoeur's phrase, the "immediacy of belief" is "irremediably lost." We half-sense that reliance upon words, in the literary sense of words understood not as charms that directly evoke what they bespeak but as symbols to be interpreted and analyzed, decolours as well as conveys that of which the words speak. In Buddhism the second and less adequate age of the Dharma, after immediacy had passed, was that of dependence upon sutras. As Ricoeur again put it, with the coming of the text, "we can no longer live the great symbolisms of the sacred in accordance with the original belief in them"; the "primitive naivete" is forever lost, and we can at best only "aim at a second naivete in and through criticism."[34]

Indeed, it may begin to dawn upon savants of the Great Tradition, as it has upon many modern critics and philosophers of language, that words of themselves fictionalize. What historical words create is not the past but a separate reality -- one may say a sub-universe -- fabricated out of a few shards from it, but which pulls and nags at humans, not because it is true, but because it is precisely other than what we know by ordinary experience to be true. This is no doubt especially true of those pasts which validate religions. Their other reality may even offer what the critic George Steiner has called a cultural equivalent of Jacques Cousteau's dizziness of the depths, an intoxicating euphoria more alluring than life on the surface.[35]

But the fact that this allure is constructed of an Indra's net of words will sooner or later also come through to those who approach the tradition mainly in terms of words. The cleavage of words from reality, though a subtle observation, is one eventually made in virtually all literate cultures. It is implied in all study of texts as texts, even

when most traditionalist. Its coming is the Great Tradition's own fore-
doomed nemesis; though its advent may take centuries or millenia, it is
embedded in the Great Tradition's own operating premises from the beginning, like hidden canker-eggs whose progeny will eventually devour their
host.

The fictionalizing quality of words does not mean, in the case of
the texts of a great religious tradition, that the original hierophany
did not happen, only that it would not have happened for its original
experiencers exactly as it portrayed in words. Something behind the
words is unrecoverable, just as "all the words in Shakespeare" cannot
fully convey the experience of anyone's average half-hour. Yet, as
these realizations arise from out of textual and intellectual labours, a
Great Tradition wearies itself in struggles against them; it is as much
from the resultant lassitude as actual disconfirmation that it loses its
grip on education, art, and its own institutionalization. Finally its
proud custodianship of the sacred words becomes an incubus it can
neither love nor shake off.

Not so with the Little Tradition. Because, as we have seen, it
essentially depends on, in the Zen phrase, "transmission outside the
scriptures" even while making a talisman of scriptures, it is spared the
verbal Saturn who devours his children. It will therefore live longer,
centuries longer, than the Great Tradition. While it obviously cannot
truly preserve the immediate experience of the first generation of the
faith, and indeed in the eye of objective history may deviate wildly
from its shape, the Little Tradition is able to produce successions of
experience which recapitulate the flavour of "primitive naiveté."

NOTES

1. Emile Durkheim, The Elementary Forms of the Religious Life. Trans. Joseph Ward Swain, New York: Collier Books, 1961 (Original French ed. 1912).

2. Bryan Wilson, "The Return of the Sacred," Journal for The Scientific Study of Religion 18: 3 (Sept. 1979), pp. 268-80.

3. Peter L. Berger, The Sacred Canopy, Garden City, NY: Doubleday and Co., 1969, p. 17.

4. Joachim Wach, The Sociology of Religion, Chicago: University of Chicago Press, 1944, pp. 17-34.

5. Thomas Luckmann, The Invisible Religion, New York: Macmillan, 1967.

6. Berger, Sacred Canopy, pp. 175-77.

7. Peter L. Berger, A Rumor of Angels, Garden City, NY: Doubleday and Co., 1970.

8. Berger, Sacred Canopy, p. 145 ff.

9. Will Herberg, Protestant, Catholic, Jew, Garden City, NY: Doubleday and Co., 1955.

10. Robert N. Bellah, The Broken Covenant, New York: Seabury Press, 1975, p. 142.

11. Berger, Sacred Canopy, p. 145.

12. Talcott Parsons, "Christianity in Modern Industrial Society," in Edward A. Tiryakin, ed., Sociological Theories, Values, and Socio-Cultural Change, New York: Free Press, 1963.

13. Andrew Greeley, Religion in the Year 2000, New York: Sheed and Ward, 1969, p. 97 ff.

14. David Martin, The Religious and the Secular, New York: Schocken Books, 1969, p. 5. Cf. Max Weber, The Sociology of Religion, trans. Ephraim Fishoff, introd. Talcott Parsons, Boston: Beacon Press, 1963 (original German source 1922), pp. xxx-xxxi (from the introduction by Talcott Parsons), and ch. 1, especially.

15. David Martin, A General Theory of Secularization, New York: Harper and Row, 1978, p. 13.

16. Ch. 7, "Secularization and the Arts: The Case of Music," and ch. 9, "The Secularization Pattern in England," in Martin, Religious and the Secular.

17. Martin, The Religious and the Secular, p. 22.

18. Martin, A General Theory of Secularization.

19. David Martin, Dilemmas of Contemporary Religion, New York: St. Martin's Press, 1978.

20. See especially Bryan Wilson, Contemporary Transformations of Religion, London: Oxford University Press, 1976.

21. Daniel Bell, "The Return of the Sacred?" British Journal of Sociology 28: 4.

22. Bryan Wilson, "The Return of the Sacred," Journal for the Scientific Study of Religion 18: 3.

23. Huston Smith, "Secularization and the Sacred: The Contemporary Scene," in Donald R. Cutler, ed., The Religious Situation 1968, Boston: Beacon Press, 1968.

24. Richard K. Fenn, Toward a Theory of Secularization. Storrs, CT: Society for the Scientific Study of Religion, Monograph Series no. 1, 1978, pp. 32-39.

25. William H. Swatos, Jr., "Beyond Denominationalism?" Journal for the Scientific Study of Religion 20: 3 (Sept 1981), pp. 217-27.

26. Religion in America 1979–80, Princeton, NJ: Princeton Religion Research Center, 1980; Religion in America: The Gallup Opinion Index 1977–78, Princeton, NJ: Gallup Opinion Index, 1978.

27. Robert Wuthnow, The Consciousness Reformation, Berkeley, CA: University of California Press, 1976.

28. Robert Redfield, Peasant Society and Culture, Chicago: University of Chicago Press, 1956, 1973, pp. 41 ff. The distinction is not new, of course; see Weber, "Castes, Estates, Classes, and Religion," Ch. 7 in his Sociology of Religion.

29. Redfield, Peasant Society and Culture, p. 46.

30. Peter W. Williams, Popular Religion in America, Englewood Cliffe, NJ: Prentice-Hall, 1980, p. 10.

31. Alfred Schutz, Collected Papers, vol. 1, edited and with an introduction by Maurice Natanson, The Hague: Martinus Nijhoff, 1973, pp. 207–59. See also William James, The Principles of Psychology, vol. 2, New York: H. Holt and Co., 1890, ch. 21.

32. See the discussion of religious "triggers" and "condensed symbols" in my Alternative Altars, Chicago: University of Chicago Press, 1979, pp. 47–49.

33. David Tracy, The Analogical Imagination: Christian Theology and the Culture of Pluralism, New York: Crossroads, 1981.

34. Paul Ricoeur, "The Symbol Gives Rise to Thought," in Giles B. Gunn, ed., Literature and Religion, New York: Harper and Row, 1971, p. 214.

35. Interview of George Steiner by Bill Moyers on broadcast of "Bill Moyers' Journal," June 1981. I am indebted to Prof. George Tanabe, Jr., for this reference.

PART II

CASE STUDIES

THE RISE OF RACISM IN THE NINETEENTH CENTURY: SYMPTOM OF MODERNITY

Alan T. Davies

The term "modernity" is a vague and ambiguous term with many connotations, both good and bad. According to the late Hannah Arendt, three
great events stood at the threshold of the modern age, predetermining
its character: "the discovery of America and the ensuing exploration of
the whole earth; the Reformation, which ... started the twofold process
of individual expropriation and the accumulation of social wealth; the
invention of the telescope and the development of a new science that
considers the nature of the earth from the viewpoint of the universe."[1]
In one sense, these events can be celebrated as tremendous transformations in the human condition that, by enlarging the spatial, social, and
intellectual perspectives of the Western mind, have extended the scope
of human freedom itself. In another sense, they can be deplored as
occasions of human alienation on an unprecedented scale for their
general effect was to shrink the world "into a Ball,"[2] stimulate capitalism together with the social horrors of the Industrial Revolution, and
reduce the human presence in the universe to utter insignificance. To
step into modernity, therefore, meant, and still means for premodern
peoples in the modern world, to step into a state of existence deeply
coloured by ambiguity in every sphere. The word is ambiguous because
the reality to which it points is ambiguous.

One symptom of this fact lies in the emergence of a series of
secular isms -- nationalism, racism, Marxism, fascism, etc -- during the
nineteenth and early twentieth centuries that have dominated the stage
of subsequent history. They also were the natural offspring of modern
alienation: a point that I shall argue later in the case of racism,
which, in various combinations with the other isms (usually with
fascism), has ravaged the earth like the proverbial devil whom God has
unchained for six millennia in Augustinian chiliasm. The immense power
that the idea of race has wielded over so large a part of the modern
consciousness until its sudden decline (but not its extinction) with the
in 1850 which glorified Saxon man as "nature's democrat" who, because of
his innate superiority over other human varieties, would someday rule
the earth. In this fashion, the myth of Anglo-Saxondom (the "Anglo" was
collapse of the German Third Reich in 1945 illustrates to a remarkable
degree the negative side of modernity. Hence, it is to this subject
that I turn.

While the term "racism" itself is recent (no older than the 1930s), racial images, particularly colour images, are extremely old in time. White Europeans intensified their feelings of racial superiority during the great age of discovery from the fifteenth to the eighteenth centuries. Even the so-called Enlightenment was tainted--as, for example, the case of David Hume, who regarded the most barbaric white as superior to the most civilized black,[3] clearly reveals. Hume, however, was scarcely a racist in the nineteenth- or twentieth-century sense, nor were his European contemporaries who adopted the same lofty attitude, because racism as a fully developed ideology arrived later on the historical scene. An ideology is more than a prejudice; it contains a system or worldview (<u>Weltanschauung</u>) by means of which everything is seen and interpreted. Once an idea acquires ideological status, it becomes the point of departure for the whole of thought, and both nature and history must be fitted into its mould. <u>Isms</u> relate to life in its entirety; hence they excite passion, and hold great numbers of people in their thrall. Moreover, the presence of passion suggests a religious element even when the <u>ism</u> assumes an anti-religious posture. This appears in the typical demand for submission to truth uttered by every ideologue, for truth implies ultimacy and religion, and if Paul Tillich is correct, is always "ultimate concern."[4] Thus the great <u>isms</u> of our <u>ism</u>-making epoch have been couched in cosmic language, such as dialectical materialism, the sacred mission of the nation, or the divinity of Aryan man. Secular religions they might be, but their power is still a religious power, as the fanaticism frequently found among their adherents clearly testifies.

The idea of race started to change itself into the ideology of racism with the writings of Robert Knox in Great Britain and Count Gobineau in France in the mid-nineteenth century. Knox, a Scottish anatomist, published a quasi-scientific work entitled <u>The Races of Men</u> added later) found scientific validation for its fast emerging role as the ideology of both the British and American peoples in their expanding power. Gobineau, a French career diplomat, published his much more famous <u>Essai sur l'inégalité des races humaines</u> in 1855, which explained the rise and fall of civilization according to racial principles. He did not invent the Aryan myth, but as no previous racial writer had done he made it the key to the entire historical process.

Human history is like an immense tapestry. The earth is the frame over which it is stretched. The successive centuries are the tireless weavers. As soon as they are born they immediately seize the shuttle and operate it on the frame, working at it until they die. The broad fabric thus goes on growing beneath their busy fingers. The two most inferior varieties of the human species, the black and yellow races, are the crude foundation, the cotton and wool, which the secondary families of the white group make supply by adding their silk; while the Aryan group, circling its finer threads through the noble generations, designs on its surface a dazzling masterpiece of arabesques in silver and gold....[5]

In both of these myths, which are really variations of the same myth, the nineteenth century white middle and upper class European painted his own self-portrait, and, like Narcissus in the ancient fable, promptly fell in love with his own reflection. The elements in this portrait are worth a moment's examination. Whiteness, of course, is an old symbol of inner purity in the European mind, but skin colour alone is not the essence of racism. Other aesthetic ideas concerning the perfect human shape that reach back into classical antiquity were incorporated into the modern European's idealization of himself, notably the straight nose, the broad forehead, the clear intelligent eyes, the athletic body suggesting harmony and balance that the Greek sculptors fashioned so magnificently.[6] These ideas were revived during the Renaissance and elevated into eternal principles by the humanists who, in their admiration of all things Greek, unwittingly supplied a model of the most beautiful type of man against which Europeans could measure other less beautiful types during the great age of discovery. Anyone who deviated from this physical norm must be inferior, and the more the American or the African deviated, the more inferior he must be.

There is nothing especially modern about narcissism per se, but it cannot be an accident that the narcissistic impulse found such powerful expression in European thought during the last century. It suggests a disorder in the modern consciousness or, as Carl Jung wrote, a spiritual vacuum that left our grandparents and great-grandparents in search of a soul.[7] Not only racism but all the great isms with which we are familiar were the products of this search, since none of them really existed during earlier periods. Nationalism, as we understand the term today, only extends back to the French Revolution (1789),[8] when the concept of the nation as a mystical entity symbolized by national flags,

national hymns, and sacred flames, etc., replaced the concept of terri-
tories pledged as personal fiefdoms to mediaeval princes and kings.
Marxism is obviously the offspring of the nineteenth century, and
fascism, a special form of nationalism, is really the child of the
twentieth century. Racism, consequently, is one sign of a larger movement arising from some kind of crisis in the Western psyche. What was
the nature of this crisis?

The English historian of ideas Michael Biddiss argues that the
secular notions of nation, class, and race arose out of the demolition
of the old Christian universe as the Age of Reason succeeded the Age of
Faith.[9] In other words, the slow process of secularization, one of the
signposts of modernity, pushed to the forefront certain ideas that
otherwise might never have found an independent place in social speculation. Each of these ideas became for certain philosophers the key to
history itself. Karl Marx isolated the concept of class as paramount;
the German romantics (e.g., Fichte)[6] isolated the concept of the nation
or Volk; Gobineau isolated the concept of race. Once these ideas
evolved into ideologies, it was only a matter of time before they were
swept into the maelstrom of modern politics. But this could never have
happened had the Christian universe with its symbols of transcendence
remained intact. Only the fragmentation of a unified vision of reality
centred on a transcendent God in which every part was linked to every
other part in a cosmic Chain of Being made it possible for the modern
mind to substitute one or other of the fragments for the God who was no
longer there. The loss of transcendence in the heavens forced our age
to locate its divinities on earth.

The older Belgian student of racist ideas, Théophile Simar, is even
more vehement. To Simar (whose study was published prior to the rise of
the German Third Reich[10]), the collapse of the beautiful, ordered,
rational universe of mediaeval Christendom was responsible for a host of
evils. Modern philosophy and theology, detached from their traditional
moorings, plunged into such dark currents as nominalism, vitalism, and
materialism. Racism is the natural product of theories that interpret
life as perpetual flux and chaotic movement, and which celebrate everlasting struggle, extreme diversity, and endless becoming. Ontological
structure, stability, and harmony have largely vanished from the modern
consciousness. Once these intellectual trends entered into the general
bloodstream of Western culture, they poisoned the entire system. Ideas
that changed themselves into ideologies during the nineteenth century
became political and national slogans during the twentieth century, and

the stage was set for the global clash of totalitarian empires.[11]

Simar, who was a nostalgic Catholic, was no doubt guilty of exaggeration both in his praise of the past and in his condemnation of the present. Yet, in spite of his exaggerations, he was probably correct in discerning a dark, ambiguous, and even immoral side to the subjectivist and vitalist currents in modern thought. It was not difficult to misread German Protestant thought in particular with its line of descent from Kant through Fichte, Schelling, Hegel, Schopenhauer, and Nietzsche as an abandonment of proper order and rationality.[12] It was not difficult to misinterpret what was happening to the modern mind as a delight in flux and change for their own sake, in which logos or reason played no part. Unlike Heraclitus of old, who recognized order as well as flux, the modern Heracliteans often seemed to recognize flux alone: their god, in Simar's eyes, was really chaos, a perpetual agitation of atoms in all possible directions, a sense of the enormous pulsing vitality of life liberated from everything except its own random laws of motion. To enjoy the kaleidoscopic beauty of the moment, to taste the strong wine of blood and temperament that nature has poured into one's veins, to feel within oneself the surge of genius, to worship the cult of force "sans limite" – these sensations emerged as the psychological companions of this worldview. Nietzsche, whom Simar especially disliked, greatly esteemed Heraclitus and based his concept of the will to power partly on the Greek philosopher.[13] While Simar clearly misjudged Nietzsche, forgetting that the latter stressed Apollonian order as well as Dionysian passion, he was nevertheless close to the truth in sensing a dangerous ambiguity in Nietzschean language. For Nietzsche, who mocked the racist rabble-rousers of his day, also wrote of the "overman" (Ubermensch), the "blond beast" (blonde Bestie) and the "master race" (Herrenrasse).

These ambiguities, however, are reflections of modernity itself, which, as I said earlier, is a highly ambiguous affair at best. Secularization has many facets, and can be regarded as both a liberating and an alienating phenomenon. The rise of racism was one manifestation of an overwhelming feeling of alienation or radical estrangement in both the personal and the social spheres of life experienced by modern world. To lose touch with ourselves at the deepest level of our being means that we must embark on a quest for our missing roots in order to be whole again, and this quest can be both creative and destructive. It can produce profound insights into the nature of human existence on the part of great thinkers: Kierkegaard, Marx, Dostoevsky, and Nietzsche; it can also produce extremism of thought and action -- what Fritz Stern has called the "politics of cultural despair"[14] -- because confusion, despair, and anger are deeply embedded in mental and spiritual anguish. Racism arose as one expression of the latter and, like its counterparts, as one attempt to cure the ills of Western civilization.

Alienation appeared in conjunction with the fateful changes at work in European society since the eighteenth century, both economic and political. The Industrial Revolution, which uprooted peasant families from the countryside and dumped them into urban misery, was a major cause. Capitalism, the profit-seeking catalyst of modern industrialization, seemed the great demon of the age to men who dreamed of a less individualistic, less ego-centred society, whether premodern or post-modern. From capitalism and its fruits arose, according to Marx and others, terrible consequences, notably "loneliness, frustration, hostility, insanity, crime"[15] -- in short, dehumanization on a new scale. Not only Marx but the romantic and racist writers denounced the new order vociferously. In their view, the deep, mysterious and holy depths of life itself, especially communal life, had been disturbed. Biddiss draws attention to the element of social alienation in Gobineau's racial philosophy;[16] the same could be said of Knox, who intensely disliked British society in the mid-nineteenth century.

In light of these feelings, it is not difficult to understand the power of the Aryan myth in a troubled period. Behind this and every race myth, Mircea Eliade has reminded us, beats the passion for "noble origin." The Aryan fashioned by Gobineau, his predecessors and successors, was at once "the 'primordial' Ancestor and noble 'hero'"; he was the "exemplary model that must be imitated in order to recover racial 'purity', physical strength, nobility, (and) the heroic 'ethics' of the glorious and creative 'beginnings'".[17] In other words, the Aryan was the white European's attempt to heal himself by re-establishing contact with the lost roots of his being. For this reason, the mythical Ancestor was laden with all the virtues that seemed to have disappeared from contemporary civilization, and which had to be recovered for the sake of social health. In the case of racism, this loss was traced to more than the new economic order; it was blamed on the political upheavals that began with the French Revolution of 1789. This revolution, and the revolution that followed in its wake, signified the collapse of an entire world-order and, while old worlds must die so that new worlds can be born, their dissolution is always an alienating experience. Our identity is intimately attached to the familiar at any time, and the sudden or even gradual dismantling of accepted symbols imperils our sense of who and what we are. The old regimes of Christian Europe were grounded in a cosmic scheme of things, and could not be razed without sending vibrations throughout the whole sacral system. Political symbols like economic symbols are fraught with psychological and religious significance. Hence revolution in the political order had at least as much to do with the rise of racism as revolution in the economic order had to do with the rise of radical socialism. Biddiss makes this clear in his analysis of Gobineau.[18]

According to Eliade, the Aryan myth appealed to Europeans who were unable to reconcile themselves to the revolutions of 1789 and 1848.[19] The losers in these struggles, usually the political reactionaries, could not resist the conclusion that the world was sinking into rack and ruin. Gobineau himself, estranged from a France that had exiled and murdered its natural rulers, the aristocrats, composed sad reflections on the impending death of civilization, although there is sufficient narcissism in his pages to suggest that his own death was the true object of his contemplation. His Essai was written during his sojourn (1849-54) as a French legate in Switzerland, where he observed the evils of democracy, associated with the hated revolutionary tradition, at close range. Democracy for him meant mobocracy, or that racial abyss at the bottom of every society where degenerate elements were poised to tear up everything noble, previous and good. Gobineau's personal and social alienation was expressed in his threefold division of humanity into white, yellow, and black races. Onto the yellow and black races -- the cotton and wool of his tapestry -- he projected the unsavoury traits of those segments of French society that he most despised: the bourgeoisie and the mob. As George L. Mosse points out,[20] the self-serving, materialistic oriental of Gobineau's imagination was really an anticapitalist's portrait of the French middle class, and the sensual violent negro was really an aristocrat's portrait of the Paris backstreets and their inhabitants. The Aryan, of course, was Gobineau himself, an idealized specimen of his own chosen social class. In glorifying the noble Aryan, the silver and gold of the tapestry, the "father of racist ideology" sought to cure his own profound unhappiness.

Knox in Great Britain was both similar and different. Personally embittered because of a scandal in his career,[21] he focused his hostility on the British monarchy as an alien symbol as Gobineau had focused on French democracy. The monarchy with its Norman origins was fit only for "dynasty-loving Celts,"[2] not for Saxons or the true English who by nature are always republicans. (The same idea, incidentally, is found in Gerrard Winstanley, the Leveller tractarian of the Cromwellian era who interpreted the civil war as both a class and a race struggle.) [23] British racism, therefore, acquired a different character, although not so different as it might seem since Gobineau also glorified Germanic liberty at least in its feudal sense, and was in his own way also a republican. What really made British racism different from continental racism was the different course of British history. No nineteenth-century empire rivalled the British Empire, and no European nation occupied the same place in the sun. When Social Darwinism infused an evolutionary faith into the Saxon, Anglo-Saxondom in both its British and American manifestations acquired a triumphal temper with the march of time. Knox himself predicted the rise of a great "republican empire" -- and Anglo-Saxon colossus -- on American soil as the apotheosis of nature's democrat, after the Norman dynasty "with its shorn constitution" had been driven from that "mighty continent." [24] Whereas Gobineau fixed his vision on the past, Knox fixed his vision on the future. One way or the other, alienation would be overcome.

Any comparison between these two strategies for overcoming the ills of the present must certainly favour the British model. As long as their historical good luck lasted, those nineteenth-century Englishmen and Americans who appropriated the liberty-loving Saxon as their primordial ancestor and noble hero really did find tremendous energy and spiritual renewal as they pursued their racial dream. Thus Charles Wentworth Dilke, another British republican, painted in 1869 a glowing picture of the twentieth century as the time when the non-Saxon nations or the "cheaper peoples" will have been reduced to the status of pygmies. "Chili [sic], La Plata, and Peru must eventually become English; the Red Indian race that now occupies those countries cannot stand against our colonies; and the future of the table-lands of Africa and that of Japan and China is as clear." [25] Not mother England but the United States, according to Dilke, is the heart of this dream, for the latter is a republic and republics comprise the essence of genuine democracy. Were not the ancient Saxons really republicans? Modern Saxondom will therefore be a vast new confederacy of Saxon republics, including Britain, which must shed its obsolete monarchy. This future confederacy will be the "greater Britain" (the title of Dilke's book) whose progress nothing can impede. Just as their racial ancestors once civilized Europe after the Dark Ages, so the latter-day Saxons will civilize and rule the earth.

Not only did this vision effect a cure for social and personal alienation, but it made the Anglo-Saxons the bearers of modernity itself in both its good and its evil aspects. Besides political democracy, Britain and America, both countries with Calvinist roots, exported capitalism, industrialization, technology, the accumulation of social wealth, and the impulse to master nature. Today, we are generally sensitive to the ambiguities inherent in these forces, but our nineteenth-century predecessors were not. The British philosopher Herbert Spencer, for example, who supplied a biological basis for the Anglo-Saxon myth by inventing the concept of the "survival of fittest," thought that human evolution was shifting from egoism to altruism. This was because the new social institutions produced by the Industrial Age would eliminate war and encourage peace and harmony among the nations, thereby pulling the human species, which had to adapt to its new environment in order to survive, in the same direction.[26] (Spencer obviously had never heard of the military-industrial complex!) Everything, consequently, was moving toward a higher and better level of self-realization, and the universe was unfolding as it should. Typical, however, of this optimistic prognosis was the conviction that the scientist had a duty to lend nature a helping hand. Does not the higher race have a moral obligation to improve its own stock for the sake of the common good? This thought impelled Darwin's cousin, Sir Francis Galton, to decipher the laws of heredity and to found the science or pseudo-science of eugenics. Who can doubt, he argued, that a race may be formed in the future "as much superior mentally and morally to the modern European, as the modern European is to the lowest of the Negro races."[27] Even the Anglo-Saxon could stand a little improvement, for Galton was much distressed by the "draggled, drudged, mean look of the mass of individuals" in English towns.[28] Was it not "monstrous" that "the race best fitted to play their part on the stage of life" should be "crowded out by the incompetent, the ailing and the desponding?"[29] If these become the main breeders, racial deterioration will set in and the Anglo-Saxon will lose his civilizing capacity.

This note of fear reveals how shallow the myth of Anglo-Saxondom always was even in its golden age. The popular image of Saxon man as the natural torch-bearer of political freedom, so dear to the hearts of nineteenth-century Englishmen and Americans, could not outlive the Victorian epoch for long. It only required a shift from triumphalism to defeatism, from optimism to pessimism, to expose once again the deeper connection between racism and alienation. To illustrate this shift, I turn to the New York Brahmin, Madison Grant, who, writing as the old era ended in the flames of the First World War, drew the same conclusions concerning civilization and its impending doom as did Gobineau many years earlier. Grant's America, invaded by an "increasing number of the weak, the broken and the mentally crippled of all races drawn from the lowest stratum of the Mediterranean basin and the Balkans, together with the hordes of the wretched, submerged populations of the Polish ghettos,"[30] was being swept towards its ruin. Must not a melting pot "allowed to boil without control" result in the extinction of "Nordic man" (a term that Grant preferred to Saxon) or the "great race"?[31] Tragically, the great race, like its original Aryan ancestor and like Cro-Magnon man, whom Grant regarded as the Nordic of his day, was now passing. Indeed, the signs of his passing were evident long ago. Was not Christ, the greatest member of the great race, who was blond and Nordic like the Olympian gods, crucified between two "brunet" thieves?[32] And today dark aliens are pouring on America's shores.

In this unhappy scenario, the essence of Gobineau's _Essai_ is reproduced. Once again, civilization is seen as suspended over a racial abyss from which nothing could save it. Once again, political democracy signified racial degeneracy because it means the "rule of the worst" (Grant's departure from Anglo-Saxon premises is radical at this point).[33] Once again, the elite have been driven from their seats of power. "Finis Americae," Grant cried, exactly as Wilhelm Marr had cried "Finis Germaniae" in 1879 when predicting the victory of Judaism over Germanism.[34] The end was at hand.

Fear of the dark alien in the traditional Anglo-Saxon nations has by no means disappeared in our own time when, if anything, the sense of lostness in the modern technocratic world grows steadily worse. In Great Britain, the ex-Tory parliamentarian Enoch Powell has uttered dire warnings against the tides of coloured immigration running from the Commonwealth into the British Isles since the Second World War. If these tides persist, Powell has declared, the fundamental character of white Britain itself might disappear. "In all of its history our nation has never known a greater danger."[35] Will not the huge numbers of ex-imperial subjects now turning Wolverhampton, Smethwick, and Birmingham into "alien territory" undermine the singular fabric of English freedom if their invasion is not checked?[36] Powell, of course, denies that he is a racist. He is only concerned to preserve the British way of life. But he argues in a familiar racist pattern. Even if born in England, racial aliens do not thereby become Englishmen, nor can they. Although "in law" the West Indian or Asian may become a citizen of the United Kingdom by birth, "in fact he is a West Indian or Asian still."[37] To be truly English means to be rooted in English soil, in the "unbroken life" of England, in authentic English instincts.[38] It is not a matter of legality but of nature. The pattern is familiar because exactly the same argument was employed by the French right ("white France") during the Dreyfus era in order to claim that Jews could not be Frenchmen.

Nor has this argument vanished in contemporary France with its own dark aliens in the form of migrant workers from other lands. In 1979 a group of young neo-Gaullist intellectuals (le Club de l'Horloge) published a book entitled La Politique du Vivant (the politics of the living)[39] that, while adopting an anti-racist stance, nevertheless resurrects classical racist ideas. Like Gobineau, whose shadow looms in the distant background, the authors believe that civilization stands in mortal peril as a consequence of egalitarianism and the Jacobin legacy of the French Revolution. Like Gobineau also, only with the advantage of pseudoscientific information unknown to their nineteenth-century mentor, they believe that a healthy society must organize itself according to hierarchical principles because that is nature's way. When nations no longer heed the biological laws of nature, they sink into decadence and perish. Since racial admixture weakens the homogeneity of a people, it weakens its distinctive culture by drowning the latter in a "mass, levelling and uprooting subculture."[40] A world without race — "la panmixie planetaire"[41] towards which we are now drifting — the book declares, represents the final stage in dehumanization because it signifies the destruction of our right to be different on which freedom, in the final analysis, always depends. Has not evolution itself given us this right? "Humanity," we are warned, "is in danger of death for having forgotten the lesson of the living."[42] A wise politics, therefore, will be a politics of the living, a politics that pays serious attention to the systems and sub-systems that comprise the biological foundations of life itself, human as well as animal. An unwise politics will ignore genetic and hereditary factors on the assumption that all human beings in all essential respects are exactly the same.

This summary does not do justice to a complex argument that quite cleverly exposes the dangers and weaknesses in the political doctrines of Rousseau and Marx, nor does it distinguish between science and pseudoscience or the legitimate and illegitimate use of contemporary genetic and sociobiological research, but that is not my concern at the moment. The important point is that a book so heavily steeped in nineteenth-century romanticism and proto-racism could have been written and published in the milieu of the late twentieth century without apology or shame. Once again, we are listening to the voices of alienation and the cry for rootedness from the lips of individuals who feel that they have lost the authentic roots of their own being. Is not the politics of the living really another example of the politics of cultural despair? Is it not reasonable to expect that there will be more works of this kind? Even today, after Auschwitz, in the post-Holocaust West, neo-racism continues to flourish in one form or another among the educated as well as the uneducated, in sophisticated circles as well as in extremist movements, in the world of ideas as well as in economic and political power structures. Not even the apparent demise of the Aryan myth as a credible account of our racial origins in the ruins of the German Third Reich has prevented the subtle rebirth of racist ideas and sentiments in Western society. Can there be a better symptom of the dark side of that ambiguous state of consciousness that we call modernity?

NOTES

1. Hannah Arendt, <u>The Human Condition</u>, New York: Doubleday Anchor Books, 1959, p. 225.

2. Arendt, <u>The Human Condition</u>, p. 227.

3. "I am apt to suspect the negroes and in general all the other species of men (for there are four or five different kinds) to be naturally inferior to the whites. There never was a civilized nation of any other complexion than white, nor even any individual eminent either in action or speculation. No ingenious manufacturer amongst them, no arts, no sciences. On the other hand, the most rude and barbarous of the whites, such as the ancient GERMANS, the present TARTARS, have still something eminent about them, in their valour, form of government, or some other particular. Such a uniform and constant difference could not happen in so many countries and ages, if nature had not made an original distinction betwixt these breeds of men...."

   Cited in Richard H. Popkin, "The Philosophical Basis of Eighteenth-Century Racism", in H.E. Pagliare, ed., <u>Racism in the Eighteenth Century</u>, Cleveland: Case Western University Press, 1973, p. 245.

4. Paul Tillich, <u>Dynamics of Faith</u>, New York: Harper & Row, 1957.

5. Cited in Michael D. Biddiss, ed., <u>Gobineau: Selected Political Writings</u>, London: Jonathan Cape, 1970, pp. 162-63.

6. George L. Mosse, <u>Toward the Final Solution</u>, New York: Howard Fertig, 1978, pp. 2-3.

7. Carl Jung, <u>Modern Man in Search of a Soul</u>, 1933.

8. Hans Kohn, <u>The Idea of Nationalism</u>, New York: Collier Books, 1967, p. 3. Of course, the <u>roots</u> of nationalism, as Kohn demonstrates throughout his long study, are older.

9. Michael D. Biddiss, Father of Racist Ideology: The Social and Political Thought of Count Gobineau, London: Weidenfeld & Nicolson, 1970, p. 104.

10. Théophile Simar, Etude critique sur la formation de la doctrine des races au XVIIIe et son expansion du XIXe siécle, Academie Royale de Belgique, classes des lettres et des sciences morales et politiques, Memoires, deuxieme serie, Tome XVl, Bruxelles: Martin Lamertin, 1922, passim.

11. Cf. Hannah Arendt, "Ideology and Terror," in The Origins of Totalitarianism, New York: Meridian Books, 1958, pp. 460-79.

12. Simar, Etude critique, p. 229.

13. Cf. Walter Kaufmann, Nietzsche: Philosopher, Psychologist, Antichrist, Princeton: Princeton University Press, 1974, p. 241.

14. Fritz Stern, The Politics of Cultural Despair, Berkeley: University of California Press, 1961.

15. Dirk J. Struik, introduction (Karl Marx), Economic and Philosophic Manuscripts of 1844, trans. Martin Milligan, New York: International Publishers, 1964, p. 50.

16. Biddiss, Father of Racist Ideology, p. 67.

17. Mircea Eliade, Myth and Reality, trans. Willard R. Task, New York: Harper Torch Books, 1963, p. 183.

18. Biddiss, Father of Racist Ideology, passim.

19. Eliade, Myth and Reality, p. 183.

20. Mosse, Toward a Final Solution, p. 53.

21. Mosse, Toward a Final Solution, p. 67.

22. Robert Knox, The Races of Men, London: Henry Renshaw, 1862, p. 5.

23. "And the last enslaving conquest which the enemy got over Israel was the Norman over England; and from that time kings, lords, judges, justices, bailiffs and the violent bitter people that are freeholders, are and have been successively. The Norman bastard William himself, his colonels, captains, inferior officers and common soldiers, who still are from that time to this day in pursuit of that victory, imprisoning, robbing and killing the poor enslaved English Israelites."

    Gerrard Winstanley, "The True Levellers' Standard Advanced," in C. Hill, ed., The Law of Freedom and Other Writings, Harrowsworth: Penguin Books, 1973, p. 78.

24. Knox, The Races of Man, p. 11.

25. Charles Wentworth Dilke, Greater Britain, Philadelphia: J.B. Lippincott, 1869, p. 347.

26. Herbert Spencer, "Militancy and Industrialism," in J.D.Y. Peel, ed., Herbert Spencer on Social Evolution: Selected Writings, Chicago: University of Chicago Press, 1972, p. 149f.

27. Francis Galton, Hereditary Genius, Gloucester, Mass: Peter Smith, 1972, p. 27.

28. Galton, Hereditary Genius, p. 395.

29. Gallon, Hereditary Genius, p. 410.

30. Madison Grant, The Passing of the Great Race, New York: Charles Scribner's Sons, 1923, p. 89.

31. Grant, The Passing of the Great Race, p. 263.

32. Grant, The Passing of the Great Race, p. 230.

33. Grant, The Passing of the Great Race, p. 79.

34. Grant, The Passing of the Great Race, p. xxxiii.

35. J. Enoch Powell, Still to Decide, John Wood, ed., London: B.T. Batsford, 1972, p. 201.

36. Powell, Still to Decide, p. 184.

37. J. Enoch Powell, Freedom and Reality, John Wood, ed., Kingswood, Surrey, 1969, p. 313.

38. Powell, Freedom and Reality, p. 340.

39. Henry de Lesquen et le Club de l'Horloge, La Politique du Vivant, Paris: Albin Michel, 1979.

40. Lesquen, La Politique du Vivant, p. 213. My translation.

41. Lesquen, La Politique du Vivant, p. 240. The authors argue further that systematic hybridization will necessitate genocide as the only means of ridding the earth of those peoples whose biocultural systems cannot be dismantled (p. 246).

42. Lesquen, La Politique du Vivant, p. 253.

MODERNITY OR REACTION IN SOUTH AFRICA: THE CASE OF AFRIKANER RELIGION [1]
Irving Hexham

INTRODUCTION

Randall G. Stokes in his paper "Afrikaner Calvinism and Economic Action: the Weber Thesis in South Africa" argues that "Afrikaner traditional religion inhibited economic change." [2] This he says "would be of limited interest, were it not for the fact that the Afrikaner's religion is Calvinist." [3] In the paper he argues that the Afrikaners are, and always have been, Calvinists [4] but in spite of this "Afrikaner Calvinism also failed to exert the pressure toward rationalization of conduct which was manifest in Europe." [5] Because South African Calvinism transformed the concept of the "Elect" into "Afrikaner" [6] it "also failed to provide the motivational nexus which made European Calvinism a revolutionary force in Western economic history." [7] Yet for him the failure of the Afrikaners to develop an entrepreneurial class, prior to the Second World War, simply affirms the truth of Weber's thesis because Afrikaner Calvinism in his view was a deviant form of Calvinism. [8]

A similar argument is propounded by Jan Loubser in "Calvinism, Equality and Inclusion: The Case of Afrikaner Calvinism," which was written for Professor Eisenstadt's book The Protestant Ethic and Modernization. Here Loubser argues that because Afrikaners were "not significantly influenced by the rationalism and naturalism of the Enlightenment nor by modern Liberalism," [9] they developed into a holy community of people [10] which preserved "Orthodox Calvinism in South Africa." [11] Like Stokes, Loubser is of the opinion that Afrikaner Calvinism does not conform to the Weberian model. But this, he claims, confirms rather than disproves the truth of Weber's thesis. [12]

The most sustained, if popular, attempt to relate the Weber thesis to South African Calvinism is to be found in W. de Klerk's book The Puritans in Africa. He develops an ideal-type methodology which enables him to compare Puritans generally with Afrikaners. Then on the basis of a sweeping review of Afrikaner history he reaches the conclusion that in fact the Weber thesis fits the Afrikaner experience very well indeed. [13] In addition to these authors, many other writers could be cited to show a general tendency to view the Afrikaners as traditional Calvinists, who, in one way or another, can be related to the Weber thesis. The basis of all these arguments is probably best stated by Sheila Patterson when she writes: "South African Calvinism grew out of the velt like an aloe, unmoved by the mellowing breezes of liberalism that blew from

Europe.... South African Calvinism moved straight out of the seventeenth century into the present day."[14] Without this basic assumption the argument about Calvinism and the Weber thesis in South Africa quickly crumbles.

In my paper "Dutch Calvinism and the Development of Afrikaner Nationalism," I raise a number of objections against what I term the "received opinion" on the relationship between Afrikaner nationalism and Calvinism.[15] There I argue that there is good reason to believe that what is today called "Afrikaner Calvinism" and regarded as "the traditional religion" of the Afrikaners is in fact a nineteenth-century import.[16] A more sustained attack upon the supposed Calvinism of the Afrikaner people is to be found in Andre du Toit's forthcoming book No Chosen People.[17] In his chapter, "The history and significance of the myth of the Calvinist origins of Afrikaner nationalism," du Toit writes: "Despite the remarkable consensus on this point among what is otherwise such diverse circles with often contrary points of view -- Afrikaner nationalists as well as their critics, scholars as well as popular writers -- the major Calvinist theses are supported neither by specific historical evidence nor by more general theoretical considerations. A critical investigation will show that there is simply no contemporary evidence for the presence among early Afrikaners of a set of popular beliefs that might be recognized as 'primitive Calvinism' nor of any ideology of a chosen people with a national mission...in contemporary accounts of travellers...before the 1850's, nor... Afrikaners themselves before the last decades of the 19th century."[18] This being the case, the arguments of Stokes, Loubser, and de Klerk crumble, leaving us the question of whether or not it is possible to relate Afrikaner religion to modernity and if so how this can be done.

This essay is an attempt to re-examine the relationship between Afrikaner religion, Calvinism, and modernity in South Africa. I will not attempt to define modernity. I am assuming a general Weberian perspective which relates increasing rationalization, industrialization, urbanization, democratic institutions, and the demystification of the world with modernity. Nor will I take Calvinism to be the "traditional religion" of Afrikaners. What I do is to draw attention to various un-Calvinistic beliefs which, prior to the Second World War, were, I believe, held by the majority of Afrikaners. These beliefs I will attempt to relate to the process of modernization and social change. I will then examine one, arguably the only, orthodox Calvinist tradition in South Africa to see whether members of that tradition were proponents or opponents of modernization in Afrikaner society. In doing this I will not be arguing that these Calvinists influenced Afrikaner society as a whole but simply asking the question of whether within their own subculture they promoted or retarded modernity. Finally, I will consider my reconstruction of Afrikaner religion in terms of Robert Redfield's concept of Great and Little Traditions.

AFRIKANER TRADITIONAL RELIGION

If Calvinism is not the traditional religion of the Afrikaners, what is? In his book Bushveld Doctor the Afrikaner poet and writer Louis Leipoldt comments, "Contrary to my expectations, I did not find my Bushveld community rabidly intolerant. They possessed a religious background in the ancestral Protestantism...but it was by no means so formalistic nor straight-laced as I had been led to believe." [19] Almost fifty years earlier Olive Schreiner, another South African writer, who like Leipoldt was the child of a Protestant minister and an agnostic, had made a similar comment on the Boers. In her short essay "The Psychology of the Boer," written in 1892, she said, "It has been said of the Boer that he is bigoted and intolerant in religious matters. That this accusation should have ever been made has always appeared to us a matter of astonishment." [20] She then goes on to describe the sceptical views held by a Boer woman she had encountered many years before. [21]

Neither Leipoldt nor Schreiner attempts to give a systematic description of Afrikaner religion. However, in both Leipoldt's Bushveld Doctor and Schreiner's The Story of an African Farm one gains an impression of the daily life and thought of a people living close to nature and far from established religion. The Story of an African Farm is generally recognized as a remarkably accurate work of fiction. In it the superstitions of Afrikaners are revealed along with the general credulity of farm people. At the same time religion and the church are strongly attacked. [22] By contrast Bushveld Doctor is a factual account of Leipoldt's own experience as Medical Inspector of Schools in the Transvaal, a post to which he was appointed in 1913. His picture of Boer life supplements and confirms that of Schreiner. They agree in their account of the superstitions and general religiosity of Afrikaners.

Leipoldt comes the closest to giving a systematic account of Afrikaner religion in a chapter entitled "Bush Magic." [23] Here he discusses traditional beliefs in ghosts, healings, prophecy, witchcraft, and magic. He points out that the first recorded case of divination at the Cape was in the time of van Riebeeck when his surgeon attempted to hex him because he refused to increase the surgeon's pay.[24] From then on, Leipoldt observes "native belief and imported superstition became allied."[25]

The process by which Afrikaner religious beliefs developed is vividly described by Leipoldt who writes, "When I was a lad I heard much about Heitsi Kabib, almost as much as I heard about Jesus, and...I was much more impressed by Heitsi. He never disputed with the doctors in the Temple, but he ran races against the sun, and he had a wonderful and alluring dog.... An old Bushman shepherd taught me to throw stones at wayside graves -- a way of propitiating Heitsi Kabib that is traditional among the Bushmen...."[26] This account of the way in which the Afrikaner child is initiated into the world of the supernatural by an old family servant was confirmed many times in my conversations with elderly Afrikaners.[27] Again and again informants told me how an African, "Bushman,"[28] or "Malay"[29] servant had instructed them in the workings of nature and ways of the world. They also told me how they would love to sneak away after the evening meal to listen to the yarns and "spook" stories told by their servants around the kitchen stove or campfire. In relating these stories the attitude of my informants varied. Some openly confessed that they knew strange forces were at work in the world and were not willing to lightly dismiss either the stories or the practices they had learned as children. Others claimed to be highly sceptical about these tales and would add comments like "the Kaffirs always believe such things" and "they were fun for children," implying that they had ceased to believe once they grew up. Another response was to admit the truth of such beliefs but to cast them aside on theological grounds with comments such as "of course, as a Christian, I know these beliefs come from the devil." Some informants, however, denied all knowledge of this type of belief while others admitted listening to spook stories as children but claimed that they had never really taken them seriously.

Ghost stories exist for popular entertainment even in highly secular cultures. It may seem strange, therefore, to argue that ghost stories are part of Afrikaner traditional religion as it existed prior to the Second World War. But once they are seen in their social context within Afrikan society their religious importance becomes clear. Afrikaner spook stories are sometimes simply entertainment. But on other occasions they have definite religious connotations. This is because the background to these stories is often African beliefs about the ancestors or beliefs of Malay origin which are derived from an Islamic culture where the jinn are a living reality. As a result Afrikaner spook stories can carry with them overtones which are definitely religious.

Very often spook stories relate to the nearness of death or the activities of malevolent spirits. Spooks are thought to appear to warn people of impending death. Frequently Afrikaners tell how shortly before the death of a loved one a spirit was seen by them or a member of their family. One old lady related how her father, who had been dead several years, appeared to her a few days before her mother's rather unexpected death. Her father assured her that he was well and that soon her mother would be joining him. He then disappeared. A few days later her mother was kicked by a horse and died.[30] Other death tales are less specific. Sometimes a light or a particular animal appears around an area warning the people that death is near. Deathbed stories also contain spook elements. Frequently people will claim to have seen ghostly figures around a deathbed. Other stories describe how the dying person looked up and asked about visitors he believed were in the room when in fact only the storyteller was present. At death the spirit is believed to leave the body and be welcomed into the next world by spirit beings who are often thought of as dead relatives.

Sometimes the spirit of a recently departed person is feared. It was thought by some that the departing spirit would be lonely and therefore tempted to return to take others with it. Thus one predikant related to me how he arrived unexpectedly at a farm where the farmer's wife had recently died. As he approached the farm unobserved he saw the farmer, his eight children, and all their African workers' wives running around the farmhouse shouting, while banging pans and tins to drive away the dead woman's spirit. This practice, he observed, was one followed by the "natives" in the area. The farmer and his family were censured by the church for this lapse into paganism but the predikant believed that the practice was probably widespread in that particular area.[31]

Apart from heralding death spooks may play tricks on people and generally create problems. They can be responsible for miscarriages of farm animals as well as of humans. In certain areas it was believed that wandering spooks would take up residence in trees or pools by the river. These areas were regarded with awe and pregnant women were warned not to go near them. It was also believed that these sites presented great danger to young girls who might be tempted to suicide by the spook.

Beliefs about spooks occupying particular places merge into related beliefs about spiritual beings and nature spirits. Certain Afrikaners seem to have believed in tree, water, and air spirits although none of my informants admitted to such beliefs. What some did say was that they had known people who held these beliefs and who took magical precautions to protect themselves from the spirits.

The most popular of these beings is the tokkelossie, which is African in origin. The tokkelossie is a small, hairy man, with immense strength and sexual power. Although informants generally dismissed this belief as a "Kaffir tale" I gained the impression that many of them had more respect for the tokkelossie than they were willing to admit. One old woman told me how she always slept on a bed raised on bricks to allow the tokkelossie to pass freely underneath. When I challenged her that she seemed to believe in its actual existence she strongly denied such a belief but said that the bricks were there to "keep the girl happy" (i.e., her African maid). However, I had the distinct impression that the bricks contributed to her own peace of mind as well. [32]

The activities of the devil were another source of popular speculation. That he existed no one was in doubt. His powers over human beings were another question. Some blamed him for misfortune while others saw his hand in world events. On occasion individuals claimed that the devil caused them to act in ways they otherwise would not. No one doubted his power to possess people and a number of informants gave examples of the devil's work in the world and power over people they knew. In one case I discovered, in archival material, a man impoverished as a result of the Second Anglo-Boer War sought to improve his fortunes by establishing a brothel. When the local church council challenged him on this matter and accused him of supporting African prostitutes he didn't deny the charge. Instead he argued that the devil had made him "fall into a sin sleep." On this basis he claimed that he was not responsible for his actions and sought the forgiveness of the community. [33]

No one claimed to know anyone who had joined forces with the devil for evil purposes although many stories exist about the living communicating with the dead. Old Bushmen were considered to be experts in the occult arts and credited with the ability to raise spirits. Although this was generally frowned upon a number of people told me that they had seen it done and were convinced of the reality of the Bushmen's powers as a result. In Bushveld Doctor, Leipoldt gives a typical description of the ways in which Bushmen were supposed to contact the dead through their appearance in the smoke of a fire. In addition to claiming to have seen an old man raise Paracelsus, Leipoldt claims that two prominent judges, Justice Morice and Chief Justice de Villiers, admitted to him that they had witnessed similar phenomenon.[34]

Almost as common as spook beliefs were beliefs about healing. These ranged from faith healing to herbal remedies and sympathetic magic. Many of these beliefs defy classification. In Paul Kruger's autobiography, Kruger tells how after a shooting accident he amputated his own thumb. Kruger explains "the wound healed very slowly...gangrene set in...black marks rose as far as the shoulder. Then they killed a goat, took out the stomach, and cut it open. I put my hand into it while it was still warm. This Boer remedy succeeded...."[35] In explaining the incident Kruger comments that the goats grazed on a river bank where many herbs grew. This he thought explained the success of the cure.

The use of the innards of animals is common in Boer folk medicine. In this it is similar to African traditional healing and one cannot help but wonder if divination practices are at work. Most informants were adamant that these remedies were purely medical and had no religious or magical overtones although one did admit that he thought that "the old people" held different views.[36] A common remedy for influenza was to skin a sheep or lamb and lay the fresh hot pelt on the chest of the sufferer. Other remedies utilized animal dung and plants for the treatment of wounds. Certain leaves were used to make herbal cigarettes which were believed to cure a variety of ills. In other cases the leaves were thrown on smouldering fires and the patient placed where he or she could inhale the fumes. This latter usage is again reminiscent of Xhosa and Zulu healing practices and probably involved an element of belief in the power of the smoke to drive out evil spirits. In a similar way the lacerating of the skin to cure influenza seems to have had overtones of releasing demons.[37]

One practice which clearly involved a belief in sympathetic magic was the traditional cure for a rupture. Henry Taylor describes this belief in his book, Doctor to Basuto, Boer and Briton. He writes: "If a case of rupture occurred, a young sapling tree was split down the middle with an axe, the two halves of the split tree were held forcibly apart, and the patient passed through between them. Then the split tree was bound together with strong twine: if the tree recovered and lived, the patient was cured, but if it died the treatment would prove of no avail."[38] Several similar treatments were reported to me by various informants although none would admit that what was actually involved was sympathetic magic. To them these were simply the "old ways" which I was assured "sometimes worked in a wonderful way."

In The Story of an African Farm, Olive Schreiner comments on the Boer love of patent medicines. As the twentieth century progressed this love seems to have grown and increasingly replaced traditional healing practices. Isidore Frack in A South African Doctor Looks Backwards -- and Forward comments on this aspect of Boer life. Writing about Afrikaner farmers he says: "He is the most credulous creature on earth.... One of the greatest evils which keeps him poor is his inordinate love for quacks and patent medicines."[39]

Frack also goes on to comment on the relationship between illness and magical beliefs. He comments, "A frequent source of chronic disease was kaffir-poison or 'kaffergif.' In the beginning I used to argue with the people that there was no such thing as kaffir poison.... Patients used to come to me, regale their symptoms...until I almost started believing in it too. A talk with an old practitioner quickly dispelled my fears, but did not help much in disabusing my patients' minds."[40]

But if Frack could not cure kaffergif by conventional means "there were the magic workers of Slamaaiers."[41] Describing their work Frack relates: "A mysterious stranger came to the homestead.... After a time spent in discussing matters of general interest, he would suddenly take a deep sniff and put on a preoccupied air...asked why he was so thoughtful, he intimated that he 'smelled' some evil spirits, who were directly responsible for his host's eye-ache, backache or stomach ache. On being asked by the wondering farmer if he could exorcize the spirits, he came down to business, and offered to affect a cure for a consideration...."[42] Frack then describes how on one occasion he witnessed such a performance where the "whole family gathered in a corner of the kraal, listening to a weird collection of incantations by the slamaaier. This part of the proceedings over, the man, followed by the audience, commenced perambulating the kraal, until he stopped suddenly, fell on his knees and commenced digging the ground with his bare hands. He brought forth three stones the size of walnuts and told his hearers in awestruck tones that these were the excreta of the devils...." After destroying these items the slamaaier pronounced the family cured.[43]

If Frack was sceptical about such cures many Afrikaners, as he admits, were not. Informants told me similar stories involving magical potents and buried charms. In one case this magic involved a Reformed minister who began to sleep whenever he attempted to read his Bible.

After consulting an "Indian doctor" his house was inspected and a small bag of "medicine" was found to be buried under the back step. Once this was destroyed the minister was able to resume his normal devotions.[44]

The consultation of slamaaiers of Indian or Malay origin is paralleled by use of African witch doctors. Although few would admit to having approached a witch doctor themselves, most informants knew people who had done so. Usually, these expeditions were to affect a cure when other means had failed. But a number were able to tell of cases where slamaaiers and witch doctors were used by Afrikaners to hex their enemies.

In the records of the Reformed Church (Gereformeerde Kerk) there are a number of cases of witchcraft dealt with by church councils in the early years of this century.[45] Between the years 1906 and 1912 cases of witchcraft seem to have been particularly troublesome. In some cases the reason for consulting a witch doctor was clearly medical.[46] In other instances, "charms" and evil intentions are indicated.[47] Usually when a church council became aware of a case of witchcraft it would call the offending party before it and explain that such practices were un-Christian and ought to cease. In one case the man concerned argued that "some people have powers which they can use to puzzle others" and declared that he could see nothing in the Bible against such powers. All he knew was that they helped him. He was disciplined by the church but remained unrepentant.[48]

So common were these beliefs in this period that in both 1910 and 1911 the Synod of the Reformed Church in the Orange Free State held discussions of the problem as did other provincial synods. The result of these discussions was that the church commissioned two elders to write a booklet outlining the biblical position on these issues to alert church members to their dangers. After this action the issue seems to have become less of a problem and is referred to only occasionally in church documents.[49]

Probably the most important and widespread of these traditional religious beliefs is the belief in second sight or the gift of prophecy. This is usually attributed to people born with a caul who are reputed to have extraordinary psychic powers.[50] Many stories are told of warnings and advice given by such people. They are able to foresee droughts and disasters as well as weddings and births. Most informants agreed that here was a phenomenon which had to be taken seriously even if they were unable to explain it in Christian terms.[51] In addition to prophetic feats I was told of various telepathic gifts attributed to farm people. One such story involved a prominent professor who told me that before the First World War he had witnessed a fellow student communicate with his brother by telepathy over several hundred miles. He claimed that the brothers had an agreement that after lunch every Sunday they would walk out into the veld where they would seat themselves under a tree and establish telepathic contact. In this way the college boy learned of doings at home far quicker than by letter. This gift, the professor maintained, had been common among country people in his youth although he recognized that few urban Afrikaners possess it today.[52]

The best known example of a man born with the caul is Nicolaas van Rensburg, the "prophet" of Lichtenburg. Van Rensburg is said to have had his first "vision" at the age of seven when he was able to assure his mother that her fears of an attack by local Africans during the absence of her husband were unfounded. He gained his reputation as a "seer" during the Second Anglo-Boer War when on commando with General de la Rey. Apart from being credited with warning the commandoes of approaching British troops, van Rensburg is said to have had a vision in 1902 where he saw "the Red Bull wounded and defeated." This vision was held to predict de la Rey's victory over British troops at the battle of Tweebos on 7 March 1902.[53]

In July 1913 he had a vision of "fire in Europe" and later "had a vision of two great bulls fighting a struggle of life and death. Their colours were red and grey, and the red one was trampled in the dust.... He also saw the number 15 against a dark cloud from which blood poured. He saw de la Rey with his head bare, coming home. Lastly he saw a carriage filled with flowers." These visions were not interpreted by van Rensburg. However, many Afrikaners took them to predict the defeat of the British by Germany and the restoration of the old republics by de la Rey.[54] In the event de la Rey died in what appears to have been the first stages of a plot to revolt against British rule. But van Rensburg's prophecies continued to haunt Afrikaners. According to South African government intelligence reports thousands of Afrikaners listened to his visions and joined the rebels in the Civil War Rebellion of 1914 as a result. In fact in the government's view the prophecies of van Rensburg were the main cause of the 1914 rebellion.[55]

After the defeat of the rebels and his capture van Rensburg returned to his farm where he continued to have his visions. Among these he is said to have foreseen the flu epidemic of 1918 and the death of General Botha in 1919. In recent years the memory of van Rensburg, who died in 1926, has been revived through the circulation of stories about prophecies he is supposed to have made predicting such things as a Black government in Rhodesia and African armies invading South Africa.[56]

Less well remembered than van Rensburg but a far more prominent Afrikaner is Johanna Brandt. She was born in 1876, the daughter of a Dutch Reformed Church minister, the Reverend N.J. van Warmelo. In 1902 she married the Reverend Louis Ernst Brandt, a minister in the Neder-duitsch Hervormde Kerk who later became its moderator -- a post he held for twenty-one years.

During the second Anglo-Boer War Mrs. Brandt lived in Pretoria where she played an important role in hiding Boer spies and organizing women to spy on British officers. She was also responsible for alerting W.T. Stead to the appalling conditions in the Irene concentration camp which resulted in a widely publicized article in his journal, The Review of Reviews. After the war she published a book, The Irene Concentration Camp, in 1904 and then her most famous book, The Petticoat Commando or Boer Women on Secret Service, in 1913. Mrs Brandt played a prominent role in Afrikaner policies by organizing women to support the National Party of General Hertzog which was founded in 1914. In 1915 she was the cofounder of the Women's National Party and became its first president.[57]

With such a solid background in the Afrikaner establishment one would expect Johanna Brandt to be a staunch upholder of Calvinist ortho-doxy. But, in fact, she wasn't. Throughout her life she took a special interest in naturopathy and traditional healing and was a practitioner of nature cures. She wrote some twenty books and pamphlets mainly on health issues. Her best known works in this area are The Fasting Book, first published in 1921, and The Grape Cure, published in 1928. Al-though all her books on healing contain religious passages her most systematic works on religion are to be found in the beginning of The Fasting Book[58] and in two explicitly religious works, The Millenium, published in 1918, and The Paraclete or Coming World Mother, published in 1936.

Johanna Brandt stands in the same prophetic tradition as Nicolaas van Rensburg. Unlike the old seer Johanna Brandt didn't simply relate her vision; she published her interpretations and made every effort to see that they were widely circulated. The Millenium is described as "a prophetic forecast," which was "the result of Prophetic Revelations made to the Writer in a Mystic Vision, on the Death of her Mother, at 'Harmony,' Pretoria, on December 7, 1916."[59]

In The Fasting Book, Johanna Brandt's basic religious framework is clearly articulated. She proposes a basically theosophical scheme which allows for the interaction of all created things on the spiritual plane. Although her language is more sophisticated than that of the salamaaier her beliefs are not. Essentially, she claims, she is expounding "the seven Hermetic principles."[60] Explaining this she says: "Many thousands of years ago the ancient Masters of Wisdom taught the mystery of the laws of the Universe. Among their number there was one who was more than man, Hermes Trismegistus, father of Occult Wisdom, founder of Astrology and the Discoverer of Alchemy. He lived long before the days of Moses and it is thought that Father Abraham was the pupil of this mighty personage."[61] Once her position is established Johanna Brandt goes on to rehabilitate "white magic."[62]

The religious views articulated in The Fasting Book are developed and related to the Christian mystical tradition in The Millenium. Throughout her writings Johanna Brandt claimed to be a Christian and a revealer of the true meaning of the Bible.[63] After developing her religious views in The Millenium she concludes with various prophecies about the future of South Africa. These concern a "dark" future and coming judgment as well as warning to the "natives" that they must not be misled and must seek to serve God by obeying their masters.[64] The prophecies begun in The Millenium are continued in The Paraclete. Here she heralds the coming "Aquarian Age" and coming of the feminine principle.[65] She extols the importance of "magnetism" and advocates the importance of special diets in healing the sick.[66]

Because of her literary gifts Johanna Brandt articulates very clearly what I would argue is the traditional religion of Afrikaners. This is not to say that she consciously developed an Afrikaner traditional religion nor that all Afrikaners would agree with her formulation of it. But simply that when her writings are compared with oral testimony about folk practices and beliefs there is a remarkable degree of agreement. In her works prophecy and healing, magic and Christianity mix to form a systematic whole which, while definitely religious, is certainly not Calvinist.

It remains to ask whether the beliefs articulated by Johanna Brandt and found in Afrikaner oral tradition are conducive to modernity or not. About this there seems little doubt. Although Johanna Brandt uses pseudoscientific terminology and at times talks about the "evolutionary process" she is essentially a reactionary opposed to modern medicine and science.[67] Similarly the prophecies of van Rensburg concern the restoration of the old republics and the turning back of the clock to a "better age."[68] Sympathetic magic, spooks, and visions all belong to a pre- or perhaps post-modern age.[69] Therefore we may safely conclude that Afrikaner traditional religion is anti-modern and a hindrance to modernity. What needs to be asked now is does this judgment also apply to Afrikaner Calvinism?

ORTHODOX CALVINISM IN SOUTH AFRICA

Calvinism scholars may dispute whether it is possible to talk about "orthodox Calvinism" and to what extent Calvinism in South Africa is true Calvinism. But whatever the scholars may say, writers like Loubser, and many others, persist in talking about Afrikaner Calvinism as "the survival of orthodox Calvinism."[70] We must ask what these writers mean by "orthodox Calvinism" and then see if a form of Calvinism that fits their description exists in South Africa and if so how it relates to modernity.

In describing Afrikaner Calvinism as "orthodox" Loubser acknowledges his debt to Sheila Patterson, who described Afrikaner Calvinism as "straight out of the seventeenth century."[71] Both Loubser and Stokes emphasize the role of predestination in forming a central tenet in Afrikaner Calvinism,[72] while W. de Klerk grounds Afrikaner Calvinism and its doctrine of predestination squarely in the Synod of Dort, 1616-18.[73] If this is the form of Calvinism which critics take to be anti-modern and a foe of modernity, to test their theses we must, if possible, identify this type of Calvinism in South Africa and then examine it to see if the claims of its critics are true or not.

Fortunately, this task is a fairly easy one. The Nederduitse Hervormde of Gereformeerde Kerk, Dutch Reformed Church, to which the majority of Afrikaners belong, cannot be regarded as "orthodox Calvinist" if predestination and an allegiance to the teachings of the Synod of Dort are taken as defining orthodoxy. In the nineteenth century the Dutch Reformed Church was strongly influenced by English evangelicalism and today remains essentially an evangelical church. The canons of Dort are part of its heritage but few ministers adhere to them or emphasize predestination in their theology.[74] Equally easy to dispose of is the Nederduitsch Hervormde Kerk, Re-formed Church, to which Johanna Brandt belonged. From its separation from the Dutch Reformed Church in 1856 to the present the Re-formed Church has been in the forefront of theological debate in South Africa. From the start it has welcomed modern theology and rejected the historic interpretation of the Synod of Dort.

In the nineteenth and early twentieth century its ministers were liberal theologians while today they are noted for their willingness to embrace the latest theological views from Europe and America.[75] Only the small Gereformeerde Kerk, the Reformed Church, can in any way be said to remain loyal to the traditions of Dort, the doctrine of predestination and anything that resembles the usual description of Afrikaner Calvinism. Founded by Dirk Postma in 1859, the Reformed Church, whose members are known as "Doppers," represents less than 10 percent of Afrikaners. Therefore, while it is not possible to relate the views of the Doppers to Afrikaner society as a whole it is at least possible to ask whether within their own community they were friends or foes of modernity.[76]

In one sense, the Doppers are anti-modern. A popular interpretation of their nickname, the "Doppers," is that it is derived from the Dutch word domper which was the device used to extinguish candles. The Doppers it is said were once known as "dompers" because they extinguished the new light of the Enlightenment and rejected modern ideas.[77] If this is true, it will be argued, it is true only in the sphere of religion. Members of the Reformed Church are anti-modern when it comes to new religious ideas and their loyalty to the teachings of Dort. Therefore, if modernity is equated with secular rationalism, they are its foes. But, if modernity can be defined in a wider context than religious belief, if it includes such things as attitudes towards education, rationality, the demystification of the world, a rejection of magic, democracy, and the acceptance of industrial civilization then it is arguable that they are advocates of modernity.

From its foundation in 1859 the Reformed Church was closely concerned with the development of Afrikaner education. Postma quickly established his own educational system based on the Dutch concept of Christian-Nationalism. With the aid of another recent immigrant from the Netherlands, Jan Lion Cachet, 1834-1910, he founded the Theological School in Burgersdorp in 1869. So that academic standards would be maintained all entrants to the Theological School had to hold a B.A.; therefore, what they called a "Literary Department" was also founded to prepare candidates for the examinations of the University of the Cape of Good Hope which was a government-run examining body in Cape Town. At the outbreak of the Second Anglo-Boer War in 1899 the Reformed Church had established over 142 schools which educated more than 3,000 children.[78]

Following the surrender of the Boer armies in 1902 the Reformed Church played an important role in the Christian Education Movement

which supported separate schools in opposition to the newly created
school system of the British authorities. When Britain gave South
Africa virtual self-government in 1907 and the majority of Christian
National Schools were absorbed into the state system, the Reformed
Church continued to advocate Christian National Education and supported
a number of schools of its own. It argued that Christian National
Education was not simply a protest device to use against a conquerer but
an educational philosophy which ought to be recognized by the government. However, the governments of General Botha refused to recognize
Christian National Education and for many years the Reformed Church
fought a lonely battle against the secular education of the state
system.[79]

Most commentators on Christian National Education have interpreted
it in ideological terms as a reactionary device to promote Afrikaner
nationalism.[80] Its practical nature is usually overlooked, because of a
concentration on ideological statements. For members of the Reformed
Church it was an ideological defence against the impact of secular
ideologies. But it was also seen as the best possible education for the
South African situation and as an alternative to the many practical
weaknesses of the state system.[81]

One of the earliest Afrikaans novels is Willem Postma's Die
Eselskakabeen first published in 1909. Postma was a Reformed Church
minister and theorist of Christian National Education. In Die
Eselskakabeen he relates the trials of a young Afrikaner who is educated
in the British system to despise his parentage and look to Britain as
the source of all goodness. At the end of the novel the hero recognizes
his folly and returns to the values of his people, vowing to create a
new South Africa where Afrikaners need not be ashamed of being Afrikaner. Apart from pointing out many obvious inconsistencies in the
State's education system, which was based on a British imperial model,
Postma attacks South African education for its impracticality. Under
the British administration South African schools had been designed to
prepare students for matriculation and university entrance. In other
words they were intended to select candidates for the civil service of a
colonial government. As a result, children were taught British history,
Latin and Greek, and other subjects designed to give them a broad
classical education. Postma argues that this was totally inappropriate
in the South African context. At the end of high school the hero
discovers "'matric' is nothing...I was too old to be a messenger boy or
farmer and too 'learned' to become a clerk, but too ill-educated to be a

teacher...to become a lawyer, Doctor or Predikant would take too long and cost too much money...."[82] As a result, after years of hard work he is left with nothing and vows that if he were ever to become a teacher he would teach "the matriculation of practical life."[83]

Similar points were made by Dirk Postma, Jr., to the Cape of Good Hope Education Commission in 1911. Postma told the commissioners that "farmers in any part of our country who want their children educated up to Standard VII, must see that their children learn Latin and other subjects useless in their line of life." To these objections the commissioners replied with obvious incredulity, "Do you mean to say that because some children ought not to be educated as professional men that there should be no Latin?"[84]

The position of Postma and other members of the Reformed Church on education is probably best represented in the 1916 report of the Commission on Elementary Education in the Orange Free State on which Postma played a prominent role. After noting the necessity of a religiously based education the commission went on to say, "Primary Education is too much a preparation for Secondary Education," and observed that the best teachers were in Secondary Schools with the result that "the great majority of the children leave school without the necessary knowledge for after life." In their view, "In future the Primary School must be the school for the nation."[85]

They criticized the system of examinations arguing, "The main object of Primary Education, therefore, 'preparation for life' it appears has been gradually lost sight of and education has become to a large extent mere cramming for examinations."[86]

To counter this tendency they proposed that if "more attention were paid to local circumstances the necessary manual training for boys and girls would find a place in every class."[87] To meet local needs the commission urged the establishment of "Farming Schools" in every district and suggested the establishment of Agricultural Colleges and Industrial Schools on the American model.[88] The commissioners' aim in all of this was to train "small farmers and their future wives in work which they will do in after life."[89] However, the emphasis was not simply on practical skills but rather on meeting the needs of the whole person. Thus they suggested: "To add to the pleasure of the future home, attention should also be devoted to the study of such subjects as music and literature."[90] In short the educational system was to move away from one based on a classical model to one which would cater for the needs of a rural community.

However, the commissioners were not simply concerned with the needs of farmers but urged the teaching of other commercial, technical, and industrial skills which would enable their children to work in towns. Thus they suggested the introduction of shorthand, typing, engineering, and electrical subjects into schools.[91]   To teach these trades local tradesmen were to be employed on a part-time basis.   In addition the commission stressed the necessity of giving girls the same type of practical education as boys.   It also proposed the creation of evening classes for adults and suggested that it was here that people could acquire more advanced education if they required it.[92]

This evidence suggests that members of the Reformed Church were in the forefront of educational reform and were in fact advocates of modernity in education.   They wished to maintain a Christian basis to education but beyond that they wanted to prepare people for the modern world.

In approaching the related problem of "poor whites," members of the Reformed Church avoided the common retreat into a desire for a rural paradise.   For them the poor white problem was soluble but only through the industrialization of South Africa.[93]   The church went to great lengths to help its poor and saw farming as one possible route.   But, farming "must be progressive.... A member of the Reformed Church is not afraid of the light of improvements," wrote one of their theologians, Dr. Hamersma, in 1913.[94]   In his view the sins of capitalism had produced socialism but this was no reason to abandon the gains of modern industry.[95]

At a local level each congregation was responsible for its own poor and in this way the church operated its own social security system which took care of the unfortunate.   Beyond the local congregation the needs of the poor were frequently discussed at provincial meetings of the church and at the National Synod.[96]   In 1916 the Cape Provincial Meeting passed a resolution that it was "a holy calling to go into business, Leviticus 25:17."   The church had a duty to help the poor and the government should help this by erecting industrial schools where "our children can learn in the fear of God all the professions, trades and paying jobs."[97]

In the Orange Free State the Provincial Meeting proposed a self-financing aid scheme to create work in 1908.[98]   Later in 1919 it was said that to make the Kingdom of God a reality the church had to help the poor.[99]

In 1917 the Reformed Church established its own commission on the poor white problem. In its report the commission declared that it was the duty neither of the church nor of the state to create work, but rather of society as a whole. Practically, it suggested, Christians must create Christian organizations which would advance education and help create work. Factories should be established as the principal means of creating new jobs and industry must be encouraged. [100]

In addition to its advocacy of education and industry the Reformed Church took a strong stand against magic and folk medicine. As already observed between 1906 and 1911 there seems to have been an epidemic of such things in many parts of South Africa. Reports of people being censured for "magic," "witchcraft," or consulting "sympathetic doctors" came in from a number of congregations and the issue was discussed at various Provincial Meetings of the church. So great was the problem that the Synod decided to produce a brochure condemning magical practices and giving biblical grounds for their avoidance. [101] In all these debates the strong rational demystifying elements of Calvinism, which Weber observed, can be seen at work. [102]

When I talked to older members of the Reformed Church many remembered the sermons of predikants against magic, witchcraft, and faith healers. These things were dismissed as anti-Christian and irrational. Calvinism was expounded as a rational system and science-endorsed provided it was "Christian in its direction." To many an emphasis on Christian science might in itself seem irrational. But for members of the Reformed Church it was not. To them Christian science meant scientific research which acknowledged God as the creator of an orderly universe based upon his laws. [103] This emphasis upon law is crucial for understanding the rational nature of the Reformed Church's theology. For them all forms of mysticism were un-Christian and anti-rational. Thus, their leading theologian J.D. du Toit could attack the Dutch Reformed Church for its "methodism" and mystical views of holiness. Such views, he argued, lead to prophetic movements and an anti-Christian syncretism. For members of the Reformed Church, God had closed his revelation. [104] Therefore, the only prophecy possible was the exposition of the Bible. For this reason members of the Reformed Church looked with horror on popular forms of prophecy and supposed "gifts" like being born with a caul. Prophets like van Rensburg and Johanna Brandt were regarded with great suspicion at least by leaders of the Reformed Church.

When all these factors are taken into consideration I think it is safe to argue that the available evidence suggests that the Reformed

Church as a Calvinist community was on balance essentially a modernizing influence in South Africa. Olive Schreiner, no friend of religion, claimed that South Africa owed its predikants a "great debt" for bringing "civilization" to a backward people.[105] More specifically, Professor John Murray of Stellenbosch University, commenting on the work of Dirk Postma in 1977, said he "has successfully combatted other prejudices and given an impulse to the cause of education among a retro- grade people."[106] These judgments are, I believe, correct. Calvinism has served in South Africa as a modernizing force in the face of an Afrikaner traditional religion which was reactionary and anti-modern. However, despite claims, Calvinism has never triumphed in South Africa and the old religion has never died. Therefore, it is necessary for us now to consider briefly Robert Redfield's concept of Great and Little Traditions.[107]

GREAT AND LITTLE TRADITIONS IN AFRIKANER RELIGION

Robert Redfield has argued that the Great Tradition of a society is the official religion as seen by its highly educated elites, usually priests and monks. The Great Tradition's version of religion is highly literate. It concentrates on the interpretation of scripture and works of philosophical theology. As a result it is transmitted through a formal education system. Its institutions are highly routinized and it produces people of rich though conventional wisdom. Because of its historical consciousness the Great Tradition takes a long view and values institutional stability. Consequently, it tends to emphasize the historical rather than the cosmic aspects of religion and prefers intel- lectual sophistication to emotional experiences. Members of the Great Tradition are lovers of learning who distrust visionaries and charisma- tic personalities.

The Little Tradition is religion as it is understood and experi- enced by ordinary people. It is essentially non-literate and rich in mythological meaning. It has little or no concern for history of formal philosophy and is oriented to cosmic rather than historical time. The Little Tradition concentrates on experience rather than theology and is transmitted through the family and local communities. Charismatic figures are highly valued while representatives of the Great Tradition are often held in awe even though their teachings are not fully under- stood or entirely obeyed. The Little Tradition centres around seasonal festivals, family events, and communal activities. In it, action rather than reflection shapes the development of belief.

Redfield emphasizes that Great and Little Traditions continually interact with each other. The Little Tradition uses the symbolism of the Great Tradition even though it accommodates the symbols to its own realities. For its part the Great Tradition's elite will look upon the Little Tradition with an ambivalent combination of admiration and contempt. At times the two traditions are in conflict, while on other occasions they support each other.

When a Great Tradition is in decline its Little Tradition can continue with a vigorous religious life until another Great Tradition seeks to impose its beliefs as the religion of the people. This situation of religious change is well illustrated by the course of religious history in Korea, where the shamanism of the Silla kings was officially replaced by Buddhism. But with the decline of Buddhism and the imposition of Confucian rituals by the Yi Dynasty shamanism once more emerged as the enduring Little Tradition. Later in the nineteenth century when Confucianism declined, Christianity entered Korea and shamanism once more reasserted its traditional role.

Among Afrikaners Calvinism represents the Great Tradition and the heritage of Dutch civilization. But soon after the settlement of the Cape in the seventeenth century a vigorous Little Tradition seems to have developed, merging elements of European folk beliefs, Malay religion, and indigenous beliefs. In the nineteenth century a missionary effort by representatives of the Great Tradition sought to reassert the influence of Calvinism in South Africa. This enterprise met with limited success but because of its literary nature came to be seen as the religion of the Afrikaners. However, the Little Tradition continued to thrive despite attempts by members of the Great Tradition to eradicate it.

In conclusion the history of South African Calvinism in the twentieth century is best understood as a continuing and not altogether successful crusade by a Great Tradition to establish itself as the dominant religious ethos of a people, the Afrikaners. Today, with the increasing secularization of Afrikaner society, I believe we are witnessing the decline of Calvinism in South Africa and the reassertion of the Little Tradition of Afrikaner folk religion. If this is so the growth of secularization in South Africa will not mean a liberalization of the society, as many have suggested, but the growth of conservative and reactionary groups nurtured on the experiential and charismatic claims of that Little Tradition.

NOTES

1. The research upon which this paper is based was made possible by a grant from the Social Science and Humanities Research Council of Canada to whom I wish to express sincere thanks.

2. Randall G. Stokes, "Afrikaner Calvinism and Economic Action," American Journal of Sociology, 81:1 (1975) p. 62.

3. Stokes, "Afrikaner Calvinism," p. 62.

4. Stokes, "Afrikaner Calvinism," p. 68.

5. Stokes, "Afrikaner Calvinism," p. 79.

6. Stokes, "Afrikaner Calvinism," p. 79.

7. Stokes, "Afrikaner Calvinism," p. 80.

8. Stokes, "Afrikaner Calvinism," p. 80.

9. Jan J. Loubser, "Calvinism, Equality and Inclusion: The Case of Afrikaner Calvinism," S.N. Eisensadt, ed., The Protestant Ethic and Modernization, New York: Basic Books, 1968, p. 372.

10. Loubser, "Calvinism," p. 373

11. Loubser, "Calvinism," p. 379.

12. Loubser, "Calvinism," p. 380.

13. W. de Klerk, The Puritans in Africa, London: Rex Collins, 1975, pp. 136-287.

14. Sheila Patterson, The Last Trek, London: Routledge and Kegan Paul, 1957, p. 178.

15. Irving Hexham, "Dutch Calvinism and the Development of Afrikaner Nationalism," African Affairs, 79:315 (April 1980) pp. 197-202.

16. Hexham, "Dutch Calvinism," pp. 202-208.

17. See now, du Toit, "No Chosen People," <u>American Historical Review</u>, 88:4, October 1983.

18. Du Toit, "No Chosen People," pp. 2-3.

19. C. Louis Leipoldt, <u>Bushveld Doctor</u>, Cape Town: Human and Rousseau, 1980, p. 57.

20. Uys Krige, <u>Olive Schreiner: A Selection</u>, Cape Town: Oxford University Press, 1968, pp. 152.

21. Krige, <u>Olive Schreiner</u>, p. 153.

22. Kringe, <u>Olive Schreiner</u>, p. 33-36.

23. Leipoldt, Bushveld Doctor, pp. 151-67.

24. Leipoldt, Bushveld Doctor, p. 153.

25. Leipoldt, Bushveld Doctor, p. 153.

26. Leipoldt, Bushveld Doctor, p. 151.

27. Much of the evidence for this paper was gathered through life-history interviews with Afrikaners in 1981. I follow standard anthropological procedure by using a pseudonym to identify specific individuals.

28. By "Bushmen" my informants meant people of mixed race who are now classified as so-called "Coloureds."

29. Malay is another term for those classified as so-called "Coloured." It implies a person descended from Malay slaves who would possibly be Moslem.

30. Mrs. van der Hex.

31. Rev. du Ploy.

32. Mrs. du Tuban.

33. Although I have documentary evidence of this I was asked by the Church Council concerned not to reveal my source of information. Apparently members of the man's family are still alive and it was felt that publication of this incident, if identified, could cause unnecessary hurt.

34. Leipoldt, Bushveld Doctor, pp. 159, 166.

35. Paul Kruger, The Memoirs of Paul Kruger, London: T. Fisher Unwin, 1902, pp. 36–37.

36. Dr. van Coy.

37. Cf. A.T. Bryant, Zulu Medicine and Medicine-men, Cape Town: C. Struik, 1966.

38. Dr. Henry Taylor, Doctor to Basuto, Boer and Briton, Cape Town: David Phillip, 1972, p. 130.

39. Isidore Frack, A South African Doctor Looks Backward--and Forward, Pretoria, Central News Agency, 1943, p. 117. In their book Afrikaners of the Kalahari, Cambridge: Cambridge University Press, 1979, Margo and Martin Russell strangely dismiss this aspect of Afrikaner society with the statement: "Afrikaners too have developed an attitude to the treatment of ill health which cannot depend on the Western expert" (p. 4.) They then briefly mention folk medicine and patent cures but do not develop this subject. By contrast B.M. du Toit in People of the Valley, Cape Town: A.A. Balkema, 1974, has an interesting discussion of folk medicine, p. 48–49, and 84–87.

40. Frack, A South African Doctor, p. 121.

41. Frack, A South African Doctor, p. 126.

42. Frack, A South African Doctor, p. 126.

43. Frack, A South African Doctor, p. 127.

44. Dr. Malon.

45. For a fuller discussion of the role of the Reformed Church in Afrikaner society and social condition in this period, see Irving Hexham, The Irony of Apartheid: The Struggle for National Independence of Afrikaner Calvinism Against British Imperialism, Toronto: Edwin Mellen Press,1981.

46. Bloemfontein Church Council, Minutes, 1/7/1910 art. 11, p.20; 4/8/10 art. 4; 10/7/1910 art. 5.

47. Burgersdorp Church Council, Minutes, 8/4/1910 art. 8; and Middleburg Church Council Minutes 29/9/1905 art. 16, art. 11.

48. Bloemfontein Church Council, Minutes 4/8/1910 art. 8.

49. Orange River Colony/Free State Provincial Synod of the Reformed (Gereformeerde) Church, 1910 art. 39; 1911 art. 15.

50. Cf. Leipoldt, Bushveld Doctor, pp. 159-60.

51. Rev. du Ploy and two other ministers of religion discussed this with me at great length, all agreeing that it presented a problem theologically but was a reality to be taken seriously.

52. Dr. van Coy.

53. Sybrand Botha, Profeet en Krygsman: die Lewensverhaul van Siener van Rensburg, Johannesburg: Die Afrikaanse Pers, n.d.

54. D.W. Kruger, The Making of a Nation, London: Macmillan, 1969, pp. 84-87.

55. Colonial Office Papers; South Africa, 537/565, 11 November 1914.

56. A collection of these "prophecies" can be found in the Ossawa Brandwag Archive at Potchefstroom University.

57. Die Transvaler, 24/1/1964; Fleur, March 1948.

58. Johanna Brandt, The Fasting Book, Bloemfontein: De Nationale Pers, 1921, pp. 11-50.

59. Johanna Brandt, The Millenium: A Prophetic Forecast, Johannesburg: privately published, 1918, p. ii.

60. Brandt, The Fasting Book, p. 24.

61. Brandt, The Fasting Book, p. 25.

62. Brandt, The Fasting Book, p. 26.

63. Brandt, The Millenium, pp. 1-7.

64. Brandt, The Millenium, pp. 91-92, 99, 104-121.

65. Johanna Brandt, The Paraclete or Coming World Mother, privately published, 1936, pp. 12-26.

66. Brandt, The Paraclete, pp. 60-66, p. 78-95.

67. Brandt, The Fasting Book, p. 11; Brandt, The Paraclete, pp. 67-73.

68. Kruger, Making of a Nation, p. 85.

69. Frack, A South African Doctor, p. 136.

70. Loubser, "Calvinism," p. 379.

71. Patterson, Last Trek, p. 178.

72. Loubser, "Calvinism," pp. 63, 72-74; Stokes, "Afrikaner Calvinism," pp. 78-80.

73. De Klerk, Puritans in Africa, pp. 6, 18, 143.

74. Cf. J. du Plessis, The Life of Andrew Murray, London: Marshal Brothers, 1919, pp. 245-49.

75. T. Dunbar Moodie, The Rise of Afrikanerdom, Berkeley: University of

California Press, 1975, p. 60.

76. Cf. Hexham, The Irony of Apartheid, for a detailed discussion of this group in the time period 1902-15.

77. Hexham, The Irony of Apartheid, pp. 61-62.

78. Hexham, The Irony of Apartheid, pp. 63-64.

79. Hexham, The Irony of Apartheid, pp. 147-164.

80. Brian Bunting, The Rise of the South African Reich, Harmondsworth, Penguin Books, 1969, pp. 224-54.

81. Willem Postma, Die Eselskakabeen, Bloemfontein: National Pers, 1909, pp. 72-82.

82. Pastma, Die Eselskakabeen, p. 82.

83. Pastma, Die Eselskakabeen, p. 82.

84. Education Commission, Minutes of Evidence, Cape Town: Government Printers, 1911, p. 1005, sec. 13824.

85. Commission on Elementary Education and Minority Report, Bloemfontein: Government Printers, 1916, p. 5.

86. Education Commission, Report, p. 6.

87. Education Commission, Report, p. 7.

88. Education Commission, Report, p. 12.

89. Education Commission, Report, p. 13.

90. Education Commission, Report, p. 13.

91. Education Commission, Report, p. 14.

92. Education Commission, Report, p. 16.

93. Willem Postma writing under the pseudonym of Dr.O'Kulis in the newspaper Vrend des Volks, 18/8/1908; article in Reformed Church newspaper Het Kerkblad, 15/12/1915; Report of Reformed Church Commission on Poor Whites, Het Westen, 13/7/1917.

94. T. Hamersma, ed., Gedenkstukken in Verband met De Nieuwe Gereformeerde Kerk Burgersdorp, Potchefstroom: Het Westen, 1913, p. 80.

95. Hamersma, Gedenkstukken, p. 78.

96. Cf. J.H. Coetzee; Die Barmhartigheidsdiens van die Gereformeerde Kerk in Suid-Afrika, 1859-1949, Potchefstroom: Pro-Rege, 1953, pp. 153-75, pp. 235-52.

97. Cape Provincial Synod Minutes, 1916, Appendix B.

98. Orange River Colony Provincial Synod, Minutes, 1908, art. 70.

99. Orange River Colony Provincial Synod, Minutes, 1909, art. 58.

100. Het Westen, 13/7/1917.

101. Cf. notes 45-49.

102. Cf. Max Weber, The Protestant Ethic and the Spirit of Capitalism, London: Unwin University Books, 1971, pp. 105, 117.

103. Cf. S.C.W. Duvenage, Die Atoomeeu--in U Lig, Potchefstroom: Potchefstroom Herald, 1969.

104. J.D. du Toit, Die Metodisme, Amsterdam: Hoveker and Wormser, 1903.

105. Krige, Olive Schreiner, p. 150.

106. John Murray, "Some Characteristics of our Fellow Colonists," Cape Monthly Magazine, December 1977, pp. 378-79.

107. Cf. Robert Redfield, Peasant Society and Culture, Chicago: University of Chicago Press, 1965.

700 YEARS AFTER NICHIREN
Shotaro Iida

A temple bell -- not huge but a small signal bell -- rings slowly but solemnly to a crescendo of rapid and sad tones, then fades into the silence of the full house of the Main Hall (hondo) of the Honmonji, a major Nichiren temple at Ikegami in metropolitan Tokyo, at exactly 8 a.m. on October 13, 1981. The huge hondo does not have an inch of space left, or rissui no yochi nashi, which literally means "no standing room for even a gimlet."

That signal bell has been ringing for the last 700 years at exactly the same month, day, time, and place, commemorating the annual deathday of Nichiren, the Buddhist prophet who died at the age of sixty, at this place at the hour of the dragon (tatsu no koku) on the thirteenth day of the tenth month in the year 1281, the fifth year of the Koan Era. [1]

During the previous two nights and well into the next morning the huge Honmonji Temple complex and the neighbouring area were full of buses for the pilgrims, literally millions of people, each beating the famous uchiwa daiko (a round fan-shaped hand drum) while chanting or shouting O-daimoku or "Namu-myoho-renge-kyo," which means "I devote myself to the Lotus Sutra," a creation of Nichiren himself. Countless Nichiren Buddhists gathered there at Ikegami, not only from all over Japan, but from overseas as well -- I saw a group of hand-drum beating Caucasian nuns of the Nihonzan Myohoji, one of the more than dozen Nichiren Buddhist groups, in the subway greeting each other: "Until next year," "See you in the States," or "See you in India." In fact, I saw some of them at the Clarks Hotel, Varanasi, India, a month later. [2] In Tokyo, all of them spent the night chanting O-daimoku with the beat of drums in their own dojo (the practice hall) at Ikegami.

Ikegami is famous for the O-eshiki (the Grand Memorial Ceremony) of the Honmonji, one of the major festivals of Tokyo today as it was in Edo of the past, which is famous for the Mando-gyoretsu or "the March of Ten Thousand Richly Decorated Lanterns." The Mando are especially bright and the march was vigorous this year, for this is the year of 700 Years After Nichiren. And the big celebration comes customarily only once in a half century, commemorating Nichiren's birth in 1222 or death in 1282. It should be noted, therefore, the above example is merely one of the numerous commemorating activities, planned and carried out with many years of preparations and countless expenditures, easily billions and billions of yen, borne by the different Nichiren groups in their own ways, not necessarily in relation to, and even competing fiercely with, each other. Because the Japanese economy has just come out of the oil-shocks, the economic climate has been favourable for such projects as temple building, renovations, publications, films, TV series, the expansion of libraries, all commemorating ostensibly and genuinely the year of 700 Years After Nichiren.

One of the prolific writers of the Japanese Buddhist masters, Nichiren did not have the energy left to afix his seal to a dictated last letter. He was cremated in the <u>Haito</u> or "Ash Tower" of Ikegami, which now forms an important part of the Ikegami Honmonji complex. Nichiren's proper tomb, where his remains are enshrined, is in Minobusan Juonji in the Yamanashi Prefecture, a half-day's driving distance from Tokyo. Though exhausted (from persistent diarrhea), Nichiren died peacefully, surrounded by his faithful supporters and disciples.

Thirty years earlier, in 1253, Nichiren had been ambushed, and had he died then, nobody would have remembered his name, for he had only just finished his twenty years of Buddhist studies. He wrote:

> I travelled to study at the temples of different provinces, in Kamakura, Kyoto, at Mount Hiei, Mount Koya, Onjoji, and others — I had one wish: that I might learn all the teachings of the Buddha which had been brought to Japan, all the discussions by bodhisattvas and commentaries by teachers. Not only were there the Kusha, Jojitsu, Ritsu, Hosso, Sanron, Kegon, Shingon, and Tendai schools, but also the ones called Zen and Jodo. Since I wanted to learn at least the central teachings, even if I did not understand the complexities of each school, I travelled extensively....[3]

He did not neglect, however, the Confucian and Japanese literary texts either, as we gather from the copious quotations from them in his writings. After all these years of studies, why was he ambushed by a local high official instead of receiving honour from the official and his old teacher and fellow students at the Kiyozumi Temple, where he was a novice? Having chanted the Daimoku toward the sunrise over the Pacific Ocean alone that afternoon, he declared his conviction, reached after twenty years of vigorous study: Truth is to be found solely in the <u>Lotus Sutra</u> and nowhere else. This naturally offended many inclu-

ding Tojo Kagenobu, the jito, or "the local head," who was a devotee of
Amida. Kagenobu took Nichiren's belief personally, and demanded a more
modified view. Nichiren's family followed suit. He, however, remained
firm in sticking to his book, the Lotus Sutra. He could not do otherwise. This led to his long exile from his home town, which may entitle
him to be considered a prophet, for it is said: "A prophet will always
be held in honour, except in his home town, and in his own family."[4]

Had he died twenty years earlier (1261) by drowning in Izu,
Nichiren would have been remembered as a fanatic who single-handedly
criticized the powerful Hojo Shogunate by directly presenting his essay
entitled the Rissho Ankokuron or "The Treatise on the Establishment of
Righteousness and the Security of the Nation," which can be divided into
chapters on 1) The Cause of Natural Disasters, 2) Scriptural Testimony
to the Cause of Natural Disasters, 3) Aspects of the Slander of the True
Teaching, 4) The Jodo Nembutsu, 5) The Cause of Calamity and Disaster,
6) Precedents for Condemnation of Heretics, 7) Countering the Calami-
ties, 8) Outlawing Heresy, 9) The Visitor's Understanding and Discussion
of the True Buddhist Country, and finally, 10) Promise of Conversion.[5]
Merely listing the chapter titles shows it is somewhat of a drastic
document, the more so if you are the target of its criticisms, of which
the most powerful are against the nation. They include the stern
warning: "The wrath of Heaven would speedily be visited upon the
country either in the form of the curse of civil war or in the shape of
the scourge of foreign invasion."[6] The reactions to the treatise were
equally drastic -- the Pure Land Buddhists tried to kill him in a night
ambush, and finally, arrested by the Shogunate, Nichiren was sent to
exile in Ito, which resulted in more of his writings, namely, the
Shi-on-sho (The Treatise on the Four Benefactions), the Kyo-ki-ji-koku-
sho (The Treatise on the Doctrine, the Capability, the Time, and the
Country), the Ken-hobo-sho (The Treatise on the Manifestation of
Disparagement of the Teaching), the Gyoja butten shugo sho (The Book on
the Buddha and Devas protecting the Practioner of the Lotus Sutra).[7]
Thus, Nichiren was not merely a Lotus Sutra devotee, but a scholarly
activist of it as well. While his actions were based on studies of the
Sutra, his actual experiences revealed to him an inner aspect of it.

Had he died ten years earlier in 1271 when he escaped execution at
a beach spot called Tatsu no Kuchi, or "Dragon's Mouth," he might have
been remembered as a rare monk who was sentenced to death for disturbing
the nation by warning of the impending Mongolian invasion. Having
escaped from the sword of the executioner by the skin of his teeth, he

was exiled (1271-74) to a desolate cemetery on a remote island called Sado in the Japan Sea, on which the cold winds from Siberia blew. There, he exclaimed, "I am the richest man in the whole of Japan."[8] In Sado he went on writing and composed a portion of the Triad Work, the Kaimoku-sho (The Treatise on the Opening of the Eyes).

After the above four major religious persecutions (Shidai-honan) and seeing that all his warnings were in vain, he left the city of Kamakura, the abode of power, and retired deep into the mountain of Minobu. His action was again according to a book, a Chinese classic wherein such an act is recommended.[9] The cold and hunger of the harsh climate of Mt. Minobu caused Nichiren to write, on his arrival on May 17th, 1274, as follows:

> I cannot describe my hunger and thirst. There is not a cup of rice for sale. I am going to die of starvation. I am sending back the disciples who accompanied me, and I shall be alone .... if this mountain seems suitable, I may stay here awhile. At any rate, I am now alone, destined to wander through all parts of Japan. If I do settle anywhere, we shall see each other again.[10]

A handful of his supporters and backers, who were mainly the average Samurai families, did not let Nichiren and his small retinue go hungry. They sent him rice, miso paste, cooking oil, sake, and some money -- barely enough to sustain him. The hopelessly optimistic Nichiren left an everlasting essay called the Minobusan Gosho (Letter from Mount Minobu), which opens with, "Makotoni Minobu san no sumika wa chihayaburu", or "Truly Minobu is a dwelling place sent from heaven by the grace of the earth-shaking gods. Even the lowly and insensitive man or woman is arrested by its beauty." He ends his essay, as an educated Japanese should, by composing a waka, which reads:

Tachiwataru	These gathering Clouds
Mino ukigumo mo	of my own shall be cleared away
Harenubeshi	By the winds from the
Taenu Minori no	Vulture Peak, (i.e.,)
Washi no Yamakaze	the Everlasting Truth of (the Lotus Sutra).

Thus, thanks to Nichiren and his followers, Mt. Minobu, the loveliest sacred mountain with a hot-spring spa called Shimobe nearby, attracts tens of thousands of visitors from all over Japan. As we shall see later on, the close proximity of Mt. Minobu to Tokyo was an important factor for the formation of the new religions of Japan today.

Nichiren was a vegetarian, as a good monk should be, and as a good Japanese, he enjoyed the warmth of sake in the cold of Minobu. In fact, he ordered and offered a toast of sake to his executioner after his ordeal was over, for the poor fellow was only trying to do his job.

Since I have been describing Nichiren as an iron-willed prophet, it is my duty to show the other side of this great man as well -- as a warm and sensitive human being. None will be left without this feeling after having read even one or two among 300 extant letters which he wrote to his supporters and disciples, letters prompted by every occasion of human encounter -- thank-you letters for gifts, highly sublimated letters to his female followers, letters of condolence, and so forth. [11] He touched the innermost chord of his supporters and disciples through his personal letters, wherein he unconditionally gave two important things: challenge and comfort. [12] On his journey to Sado Island as a prisoner after the major religious persecution (mentioned above) fell upon his group, Nichiren wrote the following immortal letter to his disciple Nichiro (1243-1320) and four others in a jail in Kamakura:

> Tomorrow I am to cross to Sado. It is cold tonight and I pity you in jail. You, my lord, have read the Lotus Sutra with body and mind and by virtue of this you will aid your father and mother, your family, and all living beings. When others read the Lotus Sutra, they read with their mouths only, with words only, and not with their minds. Even those few who do read with their minds do not practice what they read. How precious are those who read with both mind and body! The Buddha taught: "The children of the gods shall be his servants and messengers. Swords and staves shall not touch him, nor prison harm him," and it cannot be otherwise. As soon as you are released from jail, come to me quickly. We must see each other.
>
> Respectfully,
> Nichiren. [13]

What a challenge, what a comfort, in the cold eve of persecution.

As for examples of thank-you letters, the following are more famous.

> I have received the string of coins and the bamboo
> container you sent. An arrow flies by the strength of
> the bow, clouds move by strength of the dragon, men act
> by the strength of women. The visit Lord Toki paid me
> recently was due to my Lady the Nun. When you look at
> smoke, you see fire; when you look at rain, you see the
> dragon; when you look at a man, you see a woman.
> Seeing Lord Toki was like seeing my lady.... My great-
> est concern now is your illness. As I have insisted
> for these three years that you have been ill, you
> should burn moxa to recover your health. Even those
> without sickness cannot escape impermanence, but you
> are still young. You live the Lotus Sutra, so you are
> unlikely to die an untimely death. Yours surely is not
> illness due to bad karma, but even if it were, you
> could rely on the power of the Lotus Sutra. [14]

Nichiren's challenge and comfort to an ailing female disciple comes
out very clearly and nicely even in this matter-of-fact English translation. I can assure you of the strength and tenderness of Nichiren's
original writing, which alone must have hastened her full recovery.

The next is a taste of his famous thank-you letter for some sake
and herbs, which I have translated:

> I have heated sake and just took a hearty sip with the
> herbs which you kindly sent to me. I feel a fire is
> burning inside my chest. I have started sweating now,
> as though taking a nice hot bath! I can even clean my
> body with the sweat. I thank you very very much for
> this. [15]

And lastly, a letter of condolence:

> Well now, it is forty-nine days since the late Lord
> Goro passed away. Although early death is a common
> occurrence, all who have heard of this are heart-
> broken. How much the more the mother and wife must
> suffer! I sympathize with you. There are childish
> and mature children, ugly and beautiful -- but all are
> loved. He was a boy satisfactory in every way, truly

lovable. When the late Lord Ueno died in his prime, your grief was strong, and you were ready to commit suicide by fire or by water, although pregnant with this child. But you decided to wait until the baby was safe and entrust him to someone else before taking your life. Comforted by this thought, you passed fourteen or fifteen years.

Nichiren continues by comforting her:

Thinking that your coffin would be borne by your two sons, you were sustained, but in the ninth month of this year, the sun and moon were hidden by clouds, flowers were lashed by the wind. You wept, hoping it was only a long nightmare. But you were not dreaming, and the forty-nine days of mourning rushed by. "If it is true, what shall I do?" The full-blown flower lingers, while the bud has withered. The aged mother remains, while the young child is gone.

Then he challenges her:

Oh, pitiless, transient world! Give up this heartless world and serve the Lotus Sutra that Lord Goro believed in. Help him go to the indestructible, unchanging Vulture Peak Pure Land. The father is on Vulture Peak. The mother remains behind in this world. Think with sympathy and love of the late Goro who is midway between the two. Though I have much more to say, I will stop here.

With respect,

Nichiren

Reply to My Lady the Nun, Mother of Lord Ueno. [16]

Such was Nichiren, as a man. Such was his work, as a Buddhist prophet. One may oppose, rather than share, his conviction. However, one cannot help but admire his readiness for self-sacrifice to that conviction.

Having briefly described Nichiren's life and work, I shall now turn to the other half of this paper, the 700 years after him, which is a process of increasing differentiation affected by the flow of Japanese history. I propose to present this through a convenient scheme of Robert Bellah, which is defined as:

> Evolution at any system level I define as a process of increasing differentiation and complexity of organization that endows the organism, social system, or whatever the unit in question may be with greater capacity to adapt to its environment, so that it is in some sense more autonomous relative to its environment than were its less complex ancestors. [17]

This is a useful device to analyse "a process of increasing differentiation and complexity" of Nichiren Buddhism, whose evolutionary process is still going on strongly and incessantly. As I try to see the 700 years after Nichiren as falling in the time span between early modern religion and modern religion in Bellah's scheme, it would be appropriate here to give a chart of my own as a summary of Bellah's Religious Evolution.

Having prepared a table (see appendix to this chapter) or grid of Bellah's Religious Evolution, I will now proceed to discuss the 700 years after Nichiren in terms of: Religious Symbol System; Religious Action; Religious Authority; Religious Organization; and Social Implication.

RELIGIOUS SYMBOL SYSTEM

First of all, Nichiren clearly maintains "the direct relationship between the individual and transcendental reality" through the theory and practice of the Three Great Secret Teachings, which are 1) the Honzon, 2) the Daimoku, and 3) the Kaidan. This triad is the essential component among the diverse Nichiren followers.

1. Honzon -- The Fundamental Venerable [18]

The compound honzon literally means the "original noble," "fundamental venerable," or even "the principal icon in a Buddhist temple." According to Nichiren himself, however, the Honzon is the Great Mandala, or graphic symbolization of the Eternal Buddha or the Universal transcendental reality, the cosmic life force itself. From this point, it is interesting to note that Nichiren ordered his Mandala to be hung at the head of his death-bed in the Daibo, Ikegami Honmonji, for the Mandala is the symbolization of his life work. He describes the Mandala in his

<u>Kanjin Honzon Sho</u> (The Treatise on the Spiritual Introspection of Honzon) which he called, "<u>Nyorai metsugo go-gohyakusai-shi</u>" or "Revealed for the First time in the Fifth Five Hundred Years After the Tathagata's Decease," as follows:

> The august state of the Supreme Being is this: The Heavenly Shrine is floating in the sky over the world ruled by the Primeval Master, the Lord Buddha. In the Shrine is seen the Sacred Title of the Lotus of the Perfect Truth, on either side of which are seated the Buddha Sakyamuni and Probhuta-ratna, and also on the sides, at a greater distance, the four Bodhisattva leaders, the Visista-caritra and others. The Bodhisattvas like Manjusri and Maitreya are seated farther down, as attendants of the former, while the innumerable hosts of the Bodhisattvas enlightened by the manifestations of Buddha, sit around the central group, like a great crowd of people looking up toward the court nobles surrounding the throne. [19]

Thus, the whole point of chanting the <u>Daimoku</u> in front of the <u>Daimandara</u> is the adoration of the Universal Truth embodied in the person of Buddha on the one hand, and the realization of innate Buddha-nature on the other hand, which is symbolized by putting the palms of our hands together. The Soka-gakkai (the largest group of neo-Nichiren Buddhists, who will be discussed presently) so greatly emphasize the miraculous power of the <u>Itamandara</u> (the Mandala on a board) that a direct encounter with it brings tears and ecstasy to the North American and African members as well. [20] The authenticity argument -- whether it is Nichiren's own writing or not -- is one of the heated controversies among Nichiren circles today. At any rate, the style of writing of the Sacred Title is significant because of its curly and projecting strokes, a symbol of the radiant rays emitted by it.

2. <u>Daimoku -- The Title</u>

The <u>Daimoku</u> is the five or seven characters which make up the full name of the <u>Hokekyo</u>. Kishio Satomi determines the five reasons for uttering, "Namumyohorengekyo": 1) self-intuition or reflection, 2) expression of religious joy, 3) stimulation of continuous expression, 4) auto-hypnotism for inspiration, and 5) manifestation of one's standard. [21] For Abbot Nittatsu Fujii (1885-?) (= Nich-tatsu -- Nichiren monks take <u>Nichi</u>, the sun, as the first Chinese character of their <u>dharma</u>-names), the founder of the aforementioned Nihonzan Myohoji, chanting <u>Daimoku</u> with beating drum is as natural and necessary as breathing. He has been doing this this past half-century not only all over Japan, but also in the front lines of the Sino-Japanese war, and in North America, Europe, and India, while building the Stupas of the <u>Lotus Sutra</u> everywhere, with or without overcoming violent objections. For example, his Stupa in Nepal was destroyed and burned by the Nepali Government recently. A heretical Nichiren monk (outcast by the Nichiren sect), Fujii went to India in 1932 without money and with a total lack of linguistic ability in English and Hindi, in order to bring the practice of the <u>Lotus Sutra</u> back to its cradle. He "chanted" around India and Ceylon for two years beating his fan-drum incessantly. Until he met Mahatma Gandhi in 1934, the only comments he heard were "crazy Japanese monk," from the Indians, and "a national disgrace," from Japanese diplomats. Gandhi liked the Daimoku and he adopted it in his daily puja. Later on Birla, the Indian Carnegie or Ford, helped Rev. Fujii with his centres at various places in India.

It is said that Gandhi-ji liked the powerful beat of the non-violent chanting of the <u>Daimoku</u>. [22] It is also interesting to note that nineteenth-century Japanese fishermen drifting around the Pacific Ocean used to chant "Namu-amidabutsu" a million times in the morning and evening to get a meagre daily ration in their hopeless situations. However, in a more hopeful situation, they chanted "Namu-myohorengekyo," as <u>A Diary of a Captain</u> (<u>Funaosa Nikki</u>) records: "Fellow fishermen utter the <u>Nembutsu</u> unconsciously in a stormy situation, and change over to the <u>Daimoku</u> naturally after the storm is subsided!" [23] In the proper ritual of the Nichiren sect, the invocation of the Sacred Title and the contemplation of the Mandala are always combined, as the late leading Nichiren scholar, Gyokei Umada, says:

> When a man gazes at the Mandala and recites the Sacred
> Title, heart and soul, subjectivity and objectivity
> become fused into one whole, and the worshipper
> realizes in himself the excellent qualities of the
> Supreme Being, and thereby his short life is made
> eternal and his limited virtue infinite. In short,
> Sakyamuni, the Scripture of the Lotus of the Perfect
> Truth, and the worshipper, become united, in perfect
> accord, and herein lies the consummation of the creed

of the Nichiren Sect: the peace of mind of believers and religious life. The result of all this is the realization of the Buddha Land in the present state of existence. [24]

"The realization of the Buddha Land" is the topic of the next member of the Three Great Secrets.

3. Kaidan -- The Platform of Morality

The compound kaidan simply means "a place for receiving sila or moral precepts," and Japanese historical precedents are the Three State Kaidan (within the precincts of the Todaiji in Nara, the Kannonji in Chikuzen, and the Yakushiji in Shimotsuke), established by Emperor Shomu in the eighth century, Toshodaiji's Kaidan erected by the Chinese Ritsu master Ganjin, and the Endon Kaidan founded by Dengyo Daishi on Hieizan. Nichiren's kaidan is, however, neither merely a mandala nor an ordination platform in the traditional sense, but a dojo, or place for gaining enlightenment for all Japanese, including the emperors themselves, as Nichiren writes:

> When at a certain time, the union of the state law and the Buddhist Truth shall be established, and the harmony between the two completed, both sovereign and subjects will faithfully adhere to the Great Mysteries. Then the golden age, such as were the ages under the sage kings of old, will be realized in these days of degeneration and corruption, in the time of the Latter Law. Then the establishment of the Holy See will be completed, by imperial grant and the edict of the Dictator, at a spot comparable in its excellence with the Paradise of Vulture Peak. We have only to wait for the coming of the time. Then the moral law (kaiho) will be achieved in the actual life of mankind. The Holy See will then be the seat where all men of the three countries (India, China and Japan) and the whole Jambu-dvipa (world) will be initiated into the mysteries of confession and expiation; and even the great deities, Brahma and Indra, will come down into the sanctuary and participate in the initiation. [25]

Thus Nichiren emphasized the importance of an abstract kaidan as well as the concrete building of kaidan. It was in 1965 that the Sokagakkai appealed to its members for funds to erect the huge building called Shohondo in the Taisekiji complex at the foot of Mt. Fuji. Within a few weeks, more than 350 billion yen were raised — some members sold their property and life insurance policies for this historic donation. They did this because they believed the building, which was completed in 1973, would be the Kaidan itself, as prophesied by Nichiren. The other lay organization of the Taisekiji, the head temple of the Nichiren Sho-shu (called the Myoshinko), vehemently protested the Sokagakkai's claim, which gave rise to prolonged debates and even law suits by ex-members of the Sokagakkai as well. After the effusions of the moment, some demanded the return of their donations, for the Shohondo, the Gigantic Main Hall, apparently was not after all the Kaidan of Nichiren, as propagated by the president, Ikeda. This incident was the cause of a major rift between Mr. Ikeda and Abbot Nittatsu Hosoi of the Taisekiji temple, and resulted in the resignation of President Ikeda, who became kaicho and the President of the World Association of the Nichiren Shoshu. [26]

The tension between the Sokagakkai as a lay Buddhist organization and the Taisekiji as the clerical body is an indication of a characteristic, as I see it, of the religious symbol system of Modern Religion — "the symbolization is no longer the monopoly of any group of explicitly labelled religions." At the same time, one should not discredit the painstaking efforts of the traditional Nichiren monks as I have seen all over Japan, for their restoration of historic and nearly abandoned temple sites, and the maintenance and building of the new temple complex, which give cultural continuity to the rapidly changing Japanese society. For example, I have witnessed, during the past decade, the process of such restoration in the case of Myojoji, in the outskirts of Kanazawa city, not far from the northern waves of the Japan Sea. Under the tremendous effort of Abbot Kyoyu Fujii, the six hundred year old temple complex was saved from near oblivion and now, riding with the tide of the "Discover Japan" movement, this Nichiren temple has become an important asset for the cultural and religious heritage of that prefecture. [27] Moreover, I have just learned that the Abbot Fujii's next project is the renovation and expansion of the so-called Kyozuka, or the Lotus Sutra Tumulus, at the Eighth station (Hachigome) of Mt. Fuji, wherein Nichiren buried the Lotus Sutra, and Abbot Fujii's father (the late Abbot Nichijo Fujii, the former head of the Minobusan Kuonji) [28] initiated the building project thirty years ago. As I mentioned previously, the Minobusan temple complex itself, with its breathtaking natural beauty and well-kept stupendous temples, provides an excellent haven for the highly, or rather, overly industrialized Japan and its hard-working people. Their mental and spiritual health is being looked after, in addition to visits to the numerous hot springs all over Japan, through occasional visits to the various Shinto and Buddhist mountain sanctuaries like the Minobusan, where good accommodations (run by both laymen and monks) are available.

RELIGIOUS ACTION

One can easily observe "an infinitely multiplex action which replaced the simple duplex structure" in this late twentieth century, where reality is not stable but erratic, skittish, and apocalyptic. One of these multiplex actions, which no one can dismiss (though one can oppose it) is the creation of a full-fledged political party called the Komeito (the Clean Government Party), which is a political arm of the Sokagakkai (the Value Creating Association). The Sokagakkai was, in 1962, as reported by Father Henry Van Straelen, "the most vigorous, dogmatic, exclusivistic, belligerent, self-confident, and fastest growing religious group in Japan."[29] Upon encountering the Shohondo incident, the usual money and sex scandals (both founded and unfounded) involving the ex-president Ikeda which were disclosed by his former disciples, confidants, and a lawyer, their movement seems to have subsided somewhat and the place of the Sokagakkai and the Komeito has definitely stabilized in the highly industrialized democratic Japan of today.[30] Moreover, as I heard and read during my recent stay in Japan, there is talk of a possible collaboration between the Liberal Democratic Party (in power) and the Komeito. This would indeed create a new political and religious situation in Japan. The tentative collaboration hinges on the impending judgment by the court of the ex-prime minister, Kakuei Tanaka, whose possible involvement with a Lockheed scandal is in question.

It is an historical irony that the followers of Nichiren, the Komeito, dictated by twentieth-century political reality, are trying to collaborate with the dubious power of the country. Nichiren criticized the Hojo government with his Rissho Ankokuron, as I discussed earlier. His criticisms against other dominant Buddhist schools, which are "the running dogs" of power as Nichiren perceived it, were equally vehement and had formed a significant part of his teaching and writing. According to his famous slogan: "Namu Amidabutsu is the hell without interval" (Nembutsu Mugen), "Zen is the acts of the heavenly demon" (Zen Tenma), "Shingon (Tantric Buddhism) ruins the country" (Shingon Bokoku), and "the Keepers of the Hinayana precepts are the traitors to the country" (Ritsu kokuzoku). Having challenged them thus, he demanded a gigantic public debate to decide "what is the right action for the country," to establish peace under the recurring natural disasters and immediate Mongolian invasion. Nichiren cried:

> Let me face all manner of threats and temptations....
> Such temptations I shall meet unshaken, and shall
> never be allured by them, unless my principles be
> shattered by a sage's refutation of them. I will be
> the Pillar of Japan; I will be the Eyes of Japan; I
> will be the Great Vessel of Japan. Inviolable shall
> remain these oaths.[31]

Under this dharma battle cry, Nichiren tried two things:
1. Having recognized an unavoidable mutual dependency between religion and society (= State), Nichiren demanded acceptance of saddharma by the secular power.
2. Having preached his saddharma in the streets and parks of the capital, he tried to mobilize the power of the mass at the same time.

Aside from these two essential principles, other "good deeds" of the high monks are both meaningful and harmful. Zen is the acts of the demon, for Zen masters are imagining that they have peace of mind while closing their eyes to dangers and miseries. Even the compassionate and most virtuous Vinaya Master, Ryokanbo Ninsho (1217-1303) of the Gokurakuji Temple of Kamakura, Nichiren's contemporary, became the target of Nichiren's criticism. Matsunaga writes:

> Exteriorly Ninsho has a reputation of great sanctity
> as he was known to wear poor robes, eat simple food
> and engage in social work. However, his use of Jojo
> patronage and apparent eagerness to seize honours led
> many to criticize him, even pointing out the possible
> material profits he gained from his social work.
> There is no question that he was a brilliant and
> capable man, as is evinced by his management of the

Gokurakuji and it is difficult to be certain whether his detractors were sincere or motivated by jealousy.[32]

According to Hajime Nakamura, Ninsho's major achievements are:
1. Monk disciples ... more than 2740
2. Lay disciples ... numerous
3. Renovation of temples ... 83
4. Dokuyo ... 154
5. In no Keikai ... 79
6. Building the stupas ... 20
7. Donation of the entire Tripitaka ... 14 libraries
8. Establishment of sanctuaries for birds and animals
9. Construction of bridges ... 189
10. Creation of new rice fields ... 22 places (180 chobu)
11. Road construction ... 71 places
12. Digging wells ... 33
13. Health care units ... 5
14. Havens for beggars ... 5 [33]

Contrary to Ninsho's intentions, building roads and constructing bridges became the source of people's agonies. Moreover, taxing rice from other parts of the country at the harbour of Iwajima is the cause of lamentation by the common people! [34]

Although this is not the place to discuss the matter further, the socio-economic background of Nichiren's claim would be another interesting subject of enquiry. Compared with other great masters, Dogen and Shinran for example, Nichiren's religious action was extremely political in its nature. From this point of view, the creation of the Komeito is, as I maintain, along the line of Nichiren's teaching. Its actual behaviour, however, is another matter. At any rate, it is a startling development caused by an accidental combination of the small Sokagakkai created by a sixty-year-old former school teacher named Tsunesaburo Makiguchi (1981-1944) in 1930 and the small Taisekiji Temple at the southern foot of Mr. Fuji, founded by Nikko the non-compromiser, one of the six direct disciples of Nichiren himself. That is, before his death, Nichiren appointed six disciples to propagate his religious beliefs. Among them, the third elder Nikko deserted Mt. Minobu seven years after Nichiren's death as a protest against the flattering and compromising attitudes of the other five Elders (Roso) toward the Lord Hakiri in Minobu, patron of the sect. Nikko established the Taisekiji or "the Great Rock Temple," at the foot of Mt. Fuji, wherein he endeavoured to secure large tracts to establish kaidan, a kind of Holy See as mentioned above, according to Nichiren's will. And there is the controversial Shohondo, 700 years after.

RELIGIOUS AUTHORITY AND RELIGIOUS ORGANIZATION

Among the recent Nichiren Buddhist movements, the lay Buddhist movement (the aforementioned Sokagakkai is one of them, but they still maintain direct association with Taisekiji clergy) is a good example of "my mind is my church" and "I am a sect myself" quoted from Bellah, for "each individual must work out his ultimate solutions and the religious authority provides a favourable environment," which are the characteristics of both Early Modern Religion and Modern Religion in Bellah's scheme. A Japanese expression of this is Kakutaro Kubo's (1893-1944) — the founder of the Reiyukai, the womb of the new Religions in Japan — "What good is it to only listen to priests or monks?"[35]

H. Byron Earhart lists the Buddhist-derived new religions of Japan as Kodo Kyodan, Gedatsu-kai, Shinnoyen, Nyorai-kyo, Remmom-kyo, Kokuchukai, Soka-gakkai, Reiyukai, Rissho-kosikai, and Bussho-Gonen Kai.[36] One should note that these organizations, totalling well over 10 million people (one-tenth of the Japanese), are, except for Shinnoyen and Nyoraikyo, all followers of Nichiren. Moreover, excepting Kokuchukai and Sokagakkai, the rest of them are all offshoots of the Reiyukai.[37] The origin of the Nichiren lay Buddhist movement may be found in the Honmon Putsuryushu, started by an ex-Nichiren monk, Nissen Nagamatsu (1817-1890) of Kyoto. Disgusted with the corruption of monks, he returned to secular life and started the movement in both Kyoto and Takamatsu of Shikoku Island. He claimed his movement as "butsuryu" (established by the Buddha) and not "nin-ryu" (established by mere men), which is the case with the others. The knotty Nichiren doctrines were introduced to the commoners in the form of waka (Japanese poems) and emphasized the prosperity of their businesses (members were mainly small merchants and artisans) and enlightenment of their lives through the miraculous power of the Lotus Sutra itself, rather than relying on the mediating function of the monks. He divided his members into small groups, each having equal status and talking to each other on a heart-to-heart basis, which, along with healing by chanting Daimoku, attracted the populace. Because of Nagamatsu's severe criticisms of others, like

Nichiren, he was jailed three times and exiled eight times, even after the Meiji Restoration.[38] It is very important to note that these new Nichiren lay Buddhist movements contain diverse elements in the process of religious evolution. Coexisting with twentieth-century mass media techniques, the ancient shamanistic and animistic beliefs and practices wherein their enthusiasm and strength lie, are perpetually kept in place. To understand this, I suggest the following grid of Japanese culture in general.

The Japanese islands act as a sort of estuary, with several streams emptying into it. They are:

The Western Stream	Christianity, etc.
The Pan-Asian Stream	Buddhism, etc.
The Chinese Stream	Taoism, Confucianism, etc.
The Polynesian Stream	Chieftain system, etc.
The Northern Asian Stream	Ainu, Animism, Shamanism
Indigenous Stream	Shinto, Folklore, etc.

Moreover, the perpetual coexistence of these streams is a noteworthy trait, as emphasized by Robert Bellah.[39] That is to say, these new religions have the characteristics of Modern Religion from an organizational point of view; however, their actual beliefs and practices very often have the strong traits of Archaic or even Primitive Religion, as Bellah defines them. For example, the activities of the Risshokoseikai, an offshoot of the Reiyukai whose membership and vigorous worldwide operations have surpassed those of the Reiyukai, have all the elements of the diagram. As it is well documented by themselves, I shall not describe their movement here, except to mention that it was started in Tokyo by a mere milkman, Nikkyo Niwano, along with his associate Myoko Naganuma. President Nikkyo Niwano's activities are far and wide indeed: six terms as chairman of the Union of the New Religious Organization in Japan, special guest at the Second Vatican Council, two terms as chairman of the Japan Religious League, trustee of the International Association for Religious Freedom, a member of the Peace Delegation of Religious Leaders for Banning Nuclear Weapons, a participant at the first and second Asian Peace and Anti-Nuclear Arms Conference, cochairman of the first and second Asian Peace and Anti-Nuclear Arms

Conference, co-chairman of the first and second World Conference on Religion and Peace, and president of the first Asian Conference on Religion and Peace, to name but a few.

SOCIAL IMPLICATION

The characteristics of the social implication of Modern Religion, according to Bellah, are, "culture and personality are endlessly revisable, which brought a collapse of meaning and a failure of moral standards: creative innovations continue as the antidotes or fill the gap." In the foregoing, then, I have described Nichiren and his follower's movements, which are the significant elements of the Japanese religious situation today. Just as Nichiren gave challenge and comfort to his followers 700 years ago, the Nichiren followers are finding challenge and comfort in each other or through their organizations under the banner of the Daimoku, "Namumyohorengekyo." Their movements are no longer contained in Japan only. The Nichiren Shoshu of America, for example, have an active membership of over 200,000 people, all begun by an ex-Japanese policeman and part-time university student who gave strongly needed comfort and challenge to Japanese war-brides in various parts of America, supporting himself as a dish washer from time to time. He performed his mission under the directive, challenge and comfort given by Daisaku Ikeda. It is true that one of the religious traits of modern man is "my mind is my church" and "I am a sect myself," as Bellah quoted. It is also true, however, that not everyone can and is capable of having his or her own mind and own sect. Even in America many would like to follow the leader, for we are witnessing a tremendous upsurge of fundamentalists, against the prediction of the scholars of Religionswissenschaft. Seven hundred years after his death, it seems to me, Nichiren is challenging people to have their own mind and own sect in the light of truth, exemplified by his life and work, while at the same time, he is giving the leadership. As he once honestly declared, "I will be the Pillar of Japan; I will be the Eyes of Japan; I will be the Great Vessel of Japan!"[40]

Granted that some of the followers of Nichiren in Japan have a narrow view of the world, and their activities are nothing but "a storm in a glass,"[41] as is the case in most of the Japanese Buddhist's actions now. But as noted by Dr. Fujio Ikado,[42] a leading scholar of the sociology of religion in Japan, the followers of Nichiren are not doing too badly if we evaluate them in total, rather than by each subgroup. Are they, however, able to rediscover the true mission of the followers

of Nichiren in this unnerving late twentieth century? Can they change
the sound of the temple bell of Ikegami into the bell of a dawn signal-
ling a new age to come?

Those questions might be answered in another paper entitled "750
years After Nichiren" and I, unquestionably, am not the one to write it;
700 years after Nichiren, however, proves itself to be an interesting
case study of modernity and religion.

A CHART OF BELLAH'S RELIGIOUS EVOLUTION

	IDEAL CASES	A. RELIGIOUS SYMBOL SYSTEM	B. RELIGIOUS ACTION	C. RELIGIOUS AUTHORITY	D. RELIGIOUS ORGANIZATION	E. SOCIAL IMPLICATION
I Primitive Religion	Australian religions, e.g., Dinka religion.	"Dreaming"—the identification of the mythical world and the actual world.	Ritual par excellence by "participation" and "identification."	Specialized priesthoods did not exist.	Separate social structure does not exist: church and society are one.	Ritual reinforces solidarity of society and inducts young to norms of tribal behaviour.
II Archaic Religion	Africa, Polynesia and some of the New World.	More differentiation and systematized symbolism of the above in a hierarchical way.	Worship and sacrifice as the means of communication between men as subjects and gods as objects.	Upper-status group, tending to monopolize political/military power, claims superior religious status.	Failure to develop differentiated religious collectivities including adherents as well as priests.	The rationalization of traditional social structure as well as tribal behaviour by religious cosmology.
III Historic Religion	The great world religions.	The element of transcendentalism and also demythologization relative to the above.	Based on a clearly structured conception of self, action is necessary for salvation.	Emergence of religious elite via separation of political and religious elites.	Establishment of religious collectivities by separating political and religious hierarchies.	New level of tension between political and religious elite developed: growth of literacy among elite groups.
IV Early Modern Religion	Protestant Reformation and a congeries of related cases, e.g., Shinran.	The direct relation between the individual and transcendent reality.	By dropping special ascetic and devotional practices, the service of God became a total demand in every walk of life.	By rejecting papal authority, new kind of religious two-class system (elect and reprobate) appeared.	More flexible multi-centred mode of social organization based on contract and voluntary association.	Reformation gave rise to whole series of developments from economics to social science, from education to law.
V Modern Religion	Kant made a fundamental break with traditional historic religions, followed by many others.	The symbolization is no longer the monopoly of any group explicitly labeled religious.	An infinitely multiplex structure has replaced the simple duplex one.	Each individual must work out his ultimate solutions and religious authority provides favourable environment.	"My mind is my Church" and "I am a sect myself."	Culture and personality endlessly revisable bringing collapse of meaning and moral standards, but opportunity for creative innovation.

NOTES

1. For Nichiren's life and work, see Masaharu Anesaki, Nichiren, The Buddhist Prophet, London: Oxford Univ. Press; Cambridge: Harvard Univ. Press, 1916. Bruno Petzold (ed. by Shotaro Iida & Wendy Simmons) Buddhist Prophet Nichiren -- A Lotus in the Sun, Yokohama: Hokke Journal, 1978; Laurel Rasplica Rodd, Nichiren: Selected Writings, Univ. Press of Hawaii, 1980.

2. During my ten-day stay in Varanasi for the Fifth World Sanskrit Congress, I saw two large groups of the Nihonzan Myohoji pilgrims to Rajgir where the Buddha, according to their belief, preached the Lotus-Sutra.

3. Rodd, Selected Writings, p. 5. Myoho bikuni gohenji, STNI (Showa Teihon Nichiren Shonin Ibun), p. 1553.

4. Matthew 13:57; Luke 4:24.

5. The Rissho An Kokuron, in Rodd, pp 59-81.

6. STNI, vol. I. pp. 233-241; pp. 241-246; pp. 247-273, respectively.

7. STNI, p.589.

8. STNI, (Hoonjo) p. 1239.

9. Rodd, p. 114.

10. Cf. Fumio Masutani, Chosakushu (Collected Works) Tokyo: Kadokawa Shoten, 1981, vol. 8, pp. 36-59.

11. Cf. Keiichi Yanakawa, ed., Gendai Shakai to Shukyo (The Modern Society and Religion), p. 56. Charles Glock emphasizes this point too.

12. Rodd, p. 97.

13. Rodd, p. 139.

14. STNI, p. 1897.

15. Rodd, pp. 151-152.

16. Robert N. Bellah, Beyond Belief, New York: Harper & Row, 1970, p. 21.

17. For a detailed discussion, see Petzold and Iida, Nichiren, pp. 31-38.

18. Petzold and Lida, pp. 23-24.

19. They do not call themselves the Sokagakkai in the U.S. The Nichiren Shoshu of America (NSA) is a part of the International Association of the Nichiren Sho-shu.

20. See Petzold and Iida, pp. 31-38.

21. Nittatsu Fujii, Bukkyo to Heiwa (Buddhism and Peace) Tokyo: Kyoiku Shinchosha, 1966, pp. 56-90.

22. Nihonshomin seikatsushiryo shusei, vol. 5, Tokyo: Sanichi Shobo, 1968, p. 510.

23. Petzold and Iida, pp. 36-37.

24. Petzold and Iida, pp. 64-65.

25. See Koji Sugimori, "Sokagakkai Hihan" (Criticisms of the Sokagakkai), Jiyu, July and August 1981, pp. 50-60; 53-59.

26. Nichirenshu Shinbunsha, Myojoji, Tokyo: Nichirenshu Shinbunsha, 1981.

27. Cf. Showa Bukkyo Zenshu, vol. I.

28. Ken Saito, "Soka-Gakkai: Third Force in Japanese Politics?", Orient/West 7, no. 11 (Nov. 1962), p. 98.

29. Sugimori, ibid.

30. Anesaki, p. 73.

31. Daigan & Alicia Matsunaga, Foundation of Japanese Buddhism (II), Los Angeles-Tokyo: Buddhist Books International, 1976, pp. 281-282.

32. Hajime Nakamura, Nihonshukyo no Kindaisei (Modern Characteristics of Japanese Religions), collected works, vol. 8, pp. 71-73.

33. Shogumondosho, STNI, p. 354. Thanks are due to Mr. Koichi Yamaguchi and his book, Nichiren-Shonin to Ryokanbo (Saint Nichiren and Ryokanbo, nick-named, A Monk on Fire), Yokohama: Hokke Journal, 1981. As a result of conversation with him and of his book, I am now interested in the topic.

34. Tsugunari Kubo, Zaikeshugi Bukkyo no Susume (An Invitation to Laity-centred Buddhism), Tokyo: Inner Trip, 1979, p. 12.

35. H. Byron Earhart, The New Religions of Japan: A Bibliography of Western-Language Materials, Tokyo: Sophia University (1970), p. x; as for a Japanese book of this nature, see a recent excellent publication, Shinshukyo Kenkyu-chosa Handbook (A Handbook for the Studies and Research of New Religions), ed. by Junko Inoue and others, Tokyo: Yazankaku, 1981.

36. The recent studies on Reiyukai are: Hardacre, Helen, Lay Buddhism in contemporary Japan: Reiyukai Kyodan, Princeton University Press, 1984; Kubo, Katonio, Reflexions in Search of Myself, Tokyo: Sangaku Publishing Company, 1982.

37. It is interesting to study the Fuju-fuse sect also.

38. At a meeting of the American Association of Religious Studies in San Francisco a few years ago.

39. Anesaki, p. 73.

40. Yanakawa, p. 339.

41. Thanks are also due to Dr. Fujio Ikado, Professor, Tsukuba University, for spending some time answering my questions in October 1981.

MODERNITY IN ISLAMIC PERSPECTIVE
Sheila McDonough

As the non-Western nations enter the era of the industrial and scientific revolutions, the religious thinkers of the various traditions have tried, and are trying to offer leadership to their own people in the form of guidance in dealing with the challenges of modernity as they perceive them. V.S. Naipaul, the Hindu novelist from Trinidad, has recently published a volume entitled Among the Believers [1] in which he describes his travels in the Muslim world, and his meetings with a wide variety of challenges and responses which characterize the present day Muslim efforts at coming to terms with modernity.

Naipaul's Hindu background makes him more appreciative of religiousness as personal quest than as prophetic urge to transform conditions of life in the world. This limitation tends to obscure his appreciation of some facets of Muslim hopes and intentions. Nevertheless, his book provides his readers with an imaginative journey among Muslims which does cast a good deal of light onto the dreams, visions, hopes, and anxieties of Muslim believers across the world.

Muslims experienced modernity in the first instance as a shock of intrusion into their world by aggressive and rapacious foreign nations. Napoleon's invasions of Egypt at the beginning of the nineteenth century marked the beginning of an intense effort made throughout that century by European nations trying to dominate Muslim nations. Napoleon had a dream of becoming the leader of a new, enlightened Islamic civilization. The Dutch dominated Indonesia, England was in India, England and France were actively dividing up Africa. Many Europeans thought that Islamic civilization was on the verge of disappearing.

As Naipaul's book indicates, although almost 200 years have passed since the Napoleonic invasion, Muslim nations still tend to perceive Western nations as aggressive and rapacious. Modernity as a way of life mediated by Western societies therefore seems to many Muslims to produce human beings who appear to be subhuman, that is, lacking in compassion, justice, and aesthetic sensibility. Many Muslims have therefore envisaged the challenge of modernity as a problem of how to strengthen themselves so as to be able successfully to resist domination by the powers they perceive to be intrinsically hostile.

The Muslim poet-philosopher Iqbal (1876-1938) has exercised a great deal of influence over Muslims in the Indo-Pakistan subcontinent and elsewhere. Iqbal's response to the Western notion that Islam might be

on the verge of collapse was to argue that it was, rather, the Western
civilization which was on the verge of destroying itself. His argument
assumes that a truly inhuman system will self-destruct. A poem he wrote
in 1935 in response to the Italian invasion of Abyssinia indicates his
contempt for the inhumanity of imperialist greed.

Abyssinia (18th August 1935)

Those vultures of the West have yet to learn
What poisons lurk in Abyssinia's corpse,
That rotting carcase ready to fall in pieces

Civilization's zenith, nadir of virtue;
In our world pillage is the nation's trade,
Each wolf aprowl for inoffensive lambs.

Woe to the shining honour of the Church
For Rome has shivered it in the market place
Sharp-clawed, oh Holy Father, is the truth. [2]

Elsewhere he indicates that he does not see Mussolini's imperialism
as any different in kind from that of the other Western nations.

What, are crimes like Mussolini's so unheard of in
    this age?
Why should they put Europe's goodies into such a
    silly rage? [3]

In a poem discussing the prevalence of demonic forces in the modern
world, Iqbal makes clear that he sees the Western nations as fundamentally hypocritical.

Whether parliaments
Of nations meet, or Majesty holds court,
Whoever casts his eye on another's field
Is tyrant born. Have you not seen in the West
Those Demos-governments with rosy faces
And all within a blacker than Ghengiz' soul? [4]

In brief, then, modernity was experienced by Muslims as the on-
slaught of greedy nations, eager to grab whatever they could lay their

hands on. Iqbal sees them as fundamentally hypocritical because of the disparity between the value of brotherhood and justice which they affirm and the reality of their practice towards nations weaker than themselves. In as much as modernity means blackness of soul, Iqbal and many other devout Muslims want nothing to do with it. As pious Muslims, concerned to prepare their souls to meet God, blackness of soul is a doom to be avoided at all costs. The problem is thus for Muslims to strengthen themselves against the aggressors without succumbing to the vices of oppressors.

In Naipaul's travels around the Islamic world, he notes signs of anger in many places, especially in Iran. He describes the desecration of the symbols associated with the late Shah.

> It was as though the scholar in Mashhad has sent me to Firdowsi's tomb less for the sake of Firdowsi than for this evidence of the people's rage. And rage was what I saw -- more clearly in this rich, reconstructed town than in Teheran -- when we returned to Mashhad: the burnt-out buildings (among them the Broadway cinema, with its English lettering and Las Vegas facade), the ruined, burnt pedestals in the gardens without their royal statues, all the Persepolitan, pre-Islamic motifs of the Shah's architecture mocked. The holy city was also a city of rage.[5]

The note of rage is common to Iqbal's denunciation of Mussolini, and to the Iranian protest against the westernizing of the Shah. In both cases, modernity is perceived as pattern of life lacking in elemental human values, and as a mask for domination. As Nickie Keddie has noted in her recent study of the Muslim reformer Jamal-ad-Din Afghani, self-strengthening is the dominant motif of Muslim response to Western domination.[6] Muslims may differ as to how they might most effectively strengthen themselves against Western domination, but they are agreed that they must do so.

Naipaul notes in his visit to the city of Qom in Iran the existence of a medieval form of scholarship.

> The land and the street at the end of it were full of busy, black-coated figures: it was like an old print of an Oxford street scene. But here the clerical costumes

were not borrowed; here they belonged and still had
meaning; here the Islamic middle ages still lived, and
the high organization of its learning that had dazzled
men from the dark ages of Europe.[7]

Naipaul says he found it strange to find these medieval scholars
using telephones, and guarded by soldiers with machine guns.

The telephone, the secretary: the modern apparatus
seemed strange. But Khalkhali saw himself as a man of
the age. He said — this was from the Tehran Times —
"the religious leaders were trying to enforce the rule
of the Holy Prophet Mohammed in Iran. During the days
of the Prophet swords were used to fight, now they have
been replaced by Phantom aircraft." Phantoms; not
American, not the products of a foreign science but as
international as swords, part of the stock of the great
world bazaar, and rendered Islamic by purchase.[8]

This readiness to use tools from any source is characteristic of
Muslims. Muslim leaders generally affirm that the products of modern
science should be used by Muslims, since Muslims need the strength to
defend themselves, and the tools give strength. The dilemma is whether
the tools can be taken without absorbing some facets of the culture that
produced the tools. Naipaul seems to consider this latter a vain hope,
although he notes that he meets Muslims who feel that their identity is
threatened by the foreign culture.

The student on the director's left said that Islam was
the only thing that made him human. He spoke with
tenderness and conviction; and to understand what he
meant it was necessary to try to understand how, for
him, a world without the Prophet and revelation would be
a world of chaos.[9]

This student's notion that only Islam made humans human is reminiscent of Iqbal's condemnation of the inhumanity of imperialism. There
is, however, a significant difference. The student's position assumes
that the lack of humanity outside Islam is fixed and immutable. Any
contact with the outside world would therefore be polluting and

dehumanizing. Iqbal rather criticized the specific evil of greed; he said that unless the greed was stopped, the system would corrupt itself. His criticisms were aimed at specific practices and attitudes. He did not dismiss all other ways of life as intrinsically polluting.

In his book on philosophy of religion entitled The Reconstruction of Religious Thought in Islam, Iqbal urged Muslims to work for the implementation of that "spiritual democracy which is the ultimate aim of Islam."[10] For this perspective modernity poses a challenge to Muslims to do better than the West has done in implementing an egalitarian society. It proposes that the fruits of modern science should be appropriated, but that they should be used for better, more just, and more human goals than has been the case in Europe and America.

Naipaul's travels took him among Muslims in many parts of the world. He found both variety and similarity. He found a lot of rage and hope for the transformation of society. He stresses that he found an unwillingness to be part of a wider civilization. The problem still is, however, that the wider civilization has been experienced since the time of Napoleon as fundamentally greedy and hostile. Muslims still see the Western societies as tyrants trying to victimize weaker people. Therefore, self-strengthening seems to them the only way to avoid even greater victimization.

NOTES

1. V.S. Naipaul, Among the Believers London: Penguin, 1982.

2. V.O. Kiernan, trans., Poems from Iqbal, London: John Murray, 1955, p. 73.

3. Kiernan, Poems from Iqbal, p. 75.

4. Kiernan, Poems from Iqbal, p. 80.

5. Naipaul, Among the Believers, p. 71.

6. Nicki Keddie, An Islamic Response to Imperialism, Berkeley: University of California Press, 1983.

7. Naipaul, Among the Believers, p. 53.

8. Naipaul, Among the Believers, p. 40.

9. Naipaul, Among the Believers, p. 47.

10. Mohammad Iqbal, The Reconstruction of Religious Thought in Islam, Lahore: Ashraf, reprinted, 1960, p. 180.

PART III

MODERNITY AND RELIGION

UTOPIAS AND COUNTER-UTOPIAS

Moshe Amon

Some time ago, I watched a TV program on scientific experiments
directed towards extending human life. It predicted that in the very
near future we may be able, by means of genetic engineering, to extend
the life span of a human being to at least seven or eight hundred
years. Considering the rapid technological changes that affect our mode
of life, a life span of many hundreds of years is almost tantamount to
eternity. It is hard to avoid the thought that if this scientific
prediction and what it entails in the social sphere comes true, it may
herald a new kind of civilization.

Adam could have eaten from the fruit of the Tree of Life but, as we
well know, he passed up the chance. The Bible presents us with this
notion of eternal life acquired by eating some kind of fruit. It also
gives us the possibility of acquiring eternal life by another means: the
knowledge of good and the shunning of evil (Deut. 30:15). Only Adam and
Eve had the opportunity of obtaining eternal life by partaking of food,
an opportunity that lasted only a short time while they were young and
childless. According to the biblical version which has been adopted as
a tenet of Western culture, humanity at large can reach eternal life
only through right or ethical behaviour, by means of knowing and discerning good from evil.

The story of Adam and Eve is at the heart of the Western messianic
tradition and aspirations for a return of a Golden Age -- an idle life
in the Kingdom of God where human beings can be in direct contact with
God as he strolls in the garden in the cool of the day, and where they
can live forever.

The biblical narrative makes a good deal of sense when applied to
our modern situation. Had Adam and Eve chosen to eat from the Tree of
Life, they also should have opted for zero population growth or for a
very rigid system of birth control that would have limited the population according to the accommodation available in the Garden of Eden. In
this sense, eternal life is understood on an individual level, where
each person has an infinite life span.

Eternal life may also be understood as a continuous perpetuation of
the species as a unit, with no changes throughout the ages. In this
second, broader conception of eternal life, Adam and Eve would have been
expelled from the Garden of Eden to keep them from eating of the Tree of

Knowledge, because by acquiring knowledge, humanity gained the option of change.

If, today, a gene carrying the quality of long life could be implanted in all human beings, a very rigid system of birth control would have to be enforced. If the gene were implanted in only a small segment of society, those chosen would then form the group which would decide who would live longer by artificial means and who would die of natural or unnatural causes. To preserve this privilege, the group would have to prohibit the rest of society from making independent decisions. The easiest way of ensuring this would be to prohibit access to knowledge and information.

Freedom from death must necessarily lead to the abrogation of all other freedoms by most members of a society. The social order in such a society would resemble a perverted version of Plato's Republic or, more likely, something similar to Huxley's Brave New World. The ruling class, as in ancient Sumerian mythology, would be formed by those who have access to the "tablets of Fate."

Nearly sixty years ago, the Czech writer Karel Capek, who is better known for his play R.U.R. (1920) from which we borrow the term "robot," wrote a play about an actress who discovered a potion that gave her eternal life. As long as she drank it, she kept young and beautiful, a perfect woman, perfect sexual partner, perfect actress. The trouble was that — precisely because she had reached perfection in everything she had ever wished to accomplish -- she became bored and tired, and what's more, lost the ability to love or have any meaningful human relationships. All she ever wanted was to reach perfection as a performer; once she reached it, she found no more excitement in life. She therefore stopped drinking the magic potion and subsequently died old and unfulfilled.

The actress in Capek's play is a very modern person. Her life is directed not to the pursuit of knowledge, not toward understanding, but toward personal achievement. She represents a society that has failed to develop the humanistic and ethical values that are needed to balance its technological knowledge, a society that has failed to reach mental and spiritual maturity. Technical knowledge alone leads inevitably to self-destruction or at least to the destruction of the spirit. Ultimately, the members of such a society must either turn into robots or commit suicide.

The physical form of the human body -- its shape, colour, and every other hereditary attribute -- is determined by genes located on chromosomes. The chromosomes are made of DNA, and the messages encoded in the DNA are delivered outside the nucleus by mRNA units. In a somewhat similar fashion, the form, shape, and characteristics of the social body are determined by ideologies, religions, and myths. In the social sphere, messages are coded and delivered through the medium of language.

Human language is far from being a perfect vehicle for accurate messages: it is vague, unsettled, and open to myriad interpretations. Yet, by its very imperfection, language fosters creativity and acquisition of knowledge. By its very striving to reach perfection, the imperfect form is in a perpetual state of change. In contrast, perfect forms are closed, immobile, rigid. A society which believes that it has reached perfection strives to avoid change not only by controlling speech, but also by stifling all forms of communication into a rigid form of immutable slogans.

When no restrictions are laid on it, language inspires a democratic social structure by its intrinsic openness, by being open to different interpretations and change. Such an "imperfect" language inspires questions, while a language based on slogans is confined to giving answers. Like the jumping, nitrogenous media of DNA, units of language encoded as slogans can change their place in the general scheme or can be turned upside down and cause a change in the whole structure of society. Such, for instance, was Feuerbach's claim that it was man who created God in his own image.

Like an order in a military drill, once meaningful words can turn into dead signals that get a Pavlovian response with no allowance for feedback or free thought. When living language deteriorates and dries up, the life of society at large dries up as well; the social body ossifies and becomes totalitarian.

Already many of the parameters exist that are needed to establish a "death-free" society by giving some or all of its members a special gene, or through the perpetuation of the same form. Some examples are the zero population growth ideology; totalitarian regimes ruled by groups of the elect who believe they rightfully deserve the power to determine modes of life and thought; and the deterioration of human language and its replacement by error-free computer language. Already by having opted for many of the means which lead to perpetuation of the same order, we are at least partially members of an "eternal society" paving the way for a genetically engineered society.

The turning point in all this, I believe, was in the sixteenth century, in the late dawn of the modern period. The most decisive factor was removal of the medieval world view which prevented us from understanding nature as it really is. The medieval mind tried to use logic to prove the truth of the revelation, and to explain reality in terms of the expulsion from Eden. Since the Renaissance, the way has been made clear to approach the world through its own laws, rather than to try to understand it through the divine word as revealed in scripture and interpreted by the church. The fifteenth-century neo-Platonists recognized in the world the face of God and were thus able to look God "straight in the face." But because the image of God represented ultimate truth and totality of knowledge, his image was dropped in the pursuit of truth. This started the process that has eventually led us to the emergence of the post-modern era.

The road between us and the ultimate truth is veiled by myths. Whether they are poetic descriptions or the core of an established religion, these myths obscure our vision -- not to lead us astray, but mainly to protect us from the terror, fear, and awe that is likely to befall us when facing the naked truth. When we perceive the world through the veil of myth, we feel more secure and less threatened. The past becomes more meaningful, and the future is more alluring.

The naked truth embodies a very concentrated and intense form of energy; if we approach it without adequate preparation, we will likely be burned. Only a very few people who have the right attributes and knowledge can safely break out of the confines of myth. Religious taboos protect us from the devastating effects of confrontation with a higher truth by defining the borders of the "safe" area and by prohibiting us from crossing those borders.

At the same time, religions are able to guide us safely into unknown and mysterious holy territory through appropriate myths. Some of these basic myths serve as milestones on the way to the ultimate truth, but along the road they also post warning signs stating: "Danger! High voltage." Mythologies can, at one and the same time, veil the truth, protect us from its ill effects, and unveil the means to approach it. An example of this is the mythological story of Adam and Eve's expulsion from the Garden of Eden after eating from the fruit of the Tree of Knowledge of Good and Evil. Precisely because that act caused the expulsion, it is also the key for the way back in, through ethical knowledge of good and evil. A common motif in all mythological stories is that the right end can be reached through a pure heart, good deeds, and love.

A mythological story typically depicts a hierarchical structure consisting of gods, kings, and princes who allow entry into their domain only to people of good heart or to those who have the right knowledge. The progress of a mythical hero usually starts with his answer to a call and is followed by his crossing the border into the land of the unknown. He is presented with a demanding task that can be carried out only through total subordination and dedication. After the hero overcomes many obstacles, the story concludes in a special place symbolized either by its location (as on a high mountain) or by its being of a higher nature.

Before the sixteenth century, progress was conceived in hierarchical terms. Progress was defined as returning to a golden age that existed before the decline. As long as our world was thought of as being shaped by a catastrophic event that caused the fall from above, the way of redeeming the situation involved an upward climb on the slopes of mythological peaks. Even the syntax of the Indo-European languages depicts an order of classes, and the same is true of the classical ideal of social order and the Western system of power structure. [1]

All radical changes in the social and political spheres until the sixteenth century were therefore rightly termed "renaissances" while all similar changes since then have been called "revolutions." The process of stripping the past from its myths started as early as the Italian Renaissance of the fifteenth century, most probably with Lorenzo Valla, who exposed the forgery of the Donation of Constantine.

Stripped of its myths, the past tends to become meaningless. A skeleton of naked historical facts fails to arouse any emotions, and without an emotional charge, past traditions no longer hold an authoritative grip on us. Without a meaningful frame of reference, there cannot be a historical memory worth delving into to dig out building blocks for future constructions. In the sixteenth century, the hierarchical structure of language, social values, and political orders started falling apart and flattening down.

Beginning with the sixteenth century, the ideal image was sought in the future, rather than in the past. The titles of books published in that century teem with the terms "novo," "modern," "new." Since the sixteenth century, almost every downgrading of authority of any kind has been called a "revolutionary" act. When Luther toppled the authority of the Pope from the apex of the spiritual hierarchy, he also shattered the foundations of the Holy Roman Empire, since the authority of the emperor rested upon the spiritual sovereignty of the Roman Catholic Church. The eclipse of the medieval worldview also toppled down the hierarchy of science, where philosophy had ruled supreme, and permitted the rise of natural science along more democratic lines.

Spiritual, social, political, and scientific structures exploded in the sixteenth century. It was a century of protest, reformation, and counter-reformation, the rise of nation-states and vernacular languages, formation of new religious and secular orders, and the emergence of individualism. With the dissolution of the magnificent structure of the medieval world, all those who felt suffocated by it, especially those who dwelled at the lower rungs of the social ladder, were able at last to come into the open. The decline of the upper ranks of the social and spiritual pyramid allowed the lower ranks to rise. Thus started an era of great expectations: Western civilization no longer strove to find its fulfillment and its ideal image by climbing to the top, but rather by sliding down to the bottom.

The most striking feature about this change of direction is that while the words have remained the same (with a few notable exceptions like "revolution"), terms that formerly denoted one kind of behaviour have been used more and more to describe just the opposite. Plus has become minus, and minus has become plus, and while doing exactly the reverse, people have been able to go on believing that they are reaching for the same goals. Each revolution -- that is, each new recession in the top of the value-system pyramid -- has enhanced the belief that, in order to reach any form of a golden age, the bottom should be the top. With this mode of thought, the way to the top has led necessarily to the bottom. This process of gliding downhill soon acquired some eschato-logical overtones and, from a certain critical point (most likely the French Revolution), the whole process acquired a liberating and redeem-ing connotation.

Since the sixteenth century, we have thus been experiencing a slow but deliberate change in the meaning of key terms in our vocabulary, a change which during the nineteenth and twentieth centuries has become almost total. While the tops of all kinds of hierarchical orders were falling down fast, the bottom of the social pyramid did indeed rise slightly. This slight movement upward, coupled with messianic expecta-tions, gave rise to such great hopes that it made it almost impossible to notice the significant changes that were occurring in the nature of our language.

As a result, terms that trigger social action have kept their emotional charge, but have become devoid of meaning. In the twentieth century, Nazi and other fascist regimes have been called socialist; communist regimes are said to be democratic; acts of terrorists are described as social justice; Russian and Arab aggressions are termed "peace processes"; and what some call freedom, others call serfdom. The list goes on and on. Western languages have lost the ability to reflect reality. Viewed through the medium of language, life itself has become meaningless.

Nowhere were these changes more evident than in the world of utopias, which have sprung up like mushrooms after rain since the discovery of America. To understand this phenomenon, we should notice that the first settlers in America were called not pioneers, but pilgrims. The discovery of America raised great hopes for the creation of the Kingdom of God by human endeavour. In the nineteenth century, when messianic expectations reached a climax, many countries saw themselves as New Zions -- not only in the United States, but also in Canada and South Africa, and for somewhat different reasons so did people in a score of other countries, most notably Germany and Russia. As a rule, these nineteenth century utopias preserved the traditional view that the earth is a place of sin, evil, and misery, but in the place of paradise was a man-made ideal place or "no place." These utopias depicted an immutable, totalitarian regime ruled by seers (as in More or Campanella) or by scientists (Bacon). In this sense, the sixteenth century anticipated the course of the modern and even the post-modern era.

Much of what is required for a society to become "eternal" by means of genetic engineering has already become part of our culture. It has entered our culture through utopian ideologies or nostrums, and accordingly, the right to enforce their perpetuation.

The question I would raise at this point is: Why do so many modern utopias, from the time of Jonathan Swift through H.G. Wells, Aldous Huxley, George Orwell, B.F. Skinner, and a host of other writers, depict the prospects of the future in such bleak and despondent terms? Why is it that Caliban holds sway over Prospero's island, rather than Ariel?

Perhaps this conspicuous change in modern utopias comes from the fact that our present way of life seems like paradise compared to the proposed alternatives. Modern utopias are expressions of hope which turn into despair, and of despair which turns into a nightmare. In an era when extermination and concentration camps are part of day-to-day reality, the present is to a very large extent an incarnation of hell as depicted in medieval art and literature.

As the present is the gateway to the future, the content of modern utopias serves the same purpose as the inscription that Dante saw above the gates of the inferno:

> Through me lies the road to the city of grief.
> Through me lies the pathway to woe everlasting.
> Through me lies the road to the souls that are lost.
> ... I shall last forever.
> Abandon hope, all ye who enter here!

Modern utopias no longer confront a good alternative with a bad one; they despair of both, as each leads to a dead end. The myth of the expulsion from the Garden of Eden set the stage for our social order and safeguarded it by harnessing our aggressions and destructive impulses. With secularization and the emergence of the Age of Reason, we removed the aegis of this and other myths and created a world with no place for angels. Such a world is bound to be prey to monsters, fiends, and ghouls.

The change of direction which inverted the social pyramid in the sixteenth century led to the "revolt of the masses," to so-called society, and to the rise of the enigmatic concepts of "public good," "public happiness," and the belief in "progress." During the sixteenth century, Western society started to rid itself of the concept of order on which its hierarchical structure was based. This allowed the rise of individualism, but the continuing recession of the top of the hierarchical order also resulted in the fall of the classes responsible for maintaining the order. A mass of individuals who have no concept of order and who have no centre of responsibility represents a threatening and chaotic huddle. The concept of "public good" which replaced the Tree of Knowledge as a source of a new morality led to the creation of a new mythical image, the image of an all-embracing Leviathan as a new centre of responsibility. This centre is represented by a bureaucracy which replaced both angels and demons as representatives of the Supreme.

With the decline of the social, political, and religious orders, a whole world of symbols linked to those orders lost its meaning and fell apart. This world of symbols -- which served as the common denominator in the communication system of Western civilization -- has been replaced by political slogans. Unlike past symbols, which pointed toward traditional values, these modern slogans are oriented toward the future. The expectations they create, coupled with millenarian anticipations, lead to violent rejection of everything in the present as inhibiting the coming of the Future. The all-negating figure of Turgenev's in Fathers and Sons has taken the place of the tragic figure of Hamlet, while the large array of anti-heroes in the literature of the nineteenth and twentieth centuries signifies the despair of the present.

About the same time that Robert Owen introduced the word "socialism" for the first time in a description of his utopian Cooperatives (1837), there emerged a "counter-dream" — a vision of European cities laid waste by Scythians, Vandals, and Mongols. Paintings of that time depict London, Paris, and Berlin as colossal ruins.[2] About the same time that Owen tried to spread the idea of utopian colonies, Heinrich Heine was already depicting a vision of a Germany led astray on a bloodthirsty march by its special version of philosophy:

> Because of these [German] doctrines revolutionary forces
> have developed that are only waiting for the day when
> they can break out and fill the world with terror and
> with admiration. Kantians will appear who have no more
> use for piety in the physical world than in the world of
> ideas, who with sword and axe will mercilessly rummage
> around in the soil of our European culture in order to
> eradicate the last roots of the past.... But nature
> philosophers will be more terrifying than anyone
> else...the nature philosopher will be terrible; because
> he allies himself with the primitive powers of nature
> [he] can conjure up the demonic forces of ancient German
> pantheism.
>
> Don't smile at the visionary who expects in the realm of
> reality the same revolution that has taken place in the
> realm of the intellect. The thought precedes the deed
> as lightening precedes thunder. If some day you will
> hear a crash such as never has been heard before in
> world history, you will know the German thunder has
> finally reached its mark.[3]

Western civilization is now reaching its end because it has not kept enough of the past to support a viable future. We have reached this point because we have been busy for the last 500 years cutting off the heads which kept the bodies of our culture and civilization alive.

The era of revolutions which began in the sixteenth century has proved to be a violent one. Only a few took advantage of the removal of the old worldview in order to expose the laws of nature. The majority has been busily destroying the remnants of the past and executing those who lived in their structures. As we are now reaching the bottom of the social pyramid, more and more people have become involved in this process of destruction, with the result that today violence permeates every facet of our life.

Mass society has no use for history, as there is nothing in the memory of the past to support its identity and claim for power. The traditional elite, on the other hand, bases its claim for control of the social processes on the fact that it represents past traditions, values, and thought. Mass society therefore has no use for such an elite, be it an aristocracy of blood or of spirit.

Mass society is unable to preserve the traditional human values because it has no use for them. Because modernity means separation from past traditions, it has given rise to charismatic elites in the political and the religious spheres and to a scientific elite in the social domain. Neither kind of elite relies on the past, and therefore both have little use for language as a conveyor of the past into the future.

Charismatic leaders resort to demagogic language which belies any form of truth. The scientific elite, on the other hand, resorts to professional language that transmits facts but is devoid of values. So also are the scientists themselves who leave value judgments to the charismatic political elite. The charismatic elite rides on a tide of emotions raised by high expectations, but has no means of harnessing this tide except by paying off pressure groups or lashing out with police clubs. The scientific elite reveals the laws of nature, and at the same time exposes us to the immense power that those laws represent. Uninitiated into the humanistic world and the kind of knowledge that might enable them to face the truth without harm, both elites, it seems, can lead us only to destruction.

Stripped of the protection of our old culture, we stand mute, naked, and helpless at the gate to a future world whose laws will be vastly different from anything we have known. Like Oedipus, we have found the answers to the riddle of the Sphinx, murdered God in the image of our father, and coupled with our mother (matter) in the form of our material world. Pride had driven us to play the role of the creator and our punishment is to live in the world we have created. Compared with the prospects of the future, our present may seem like paradise, but as we have already taken a very big bite out of the Tree of Knowledge, our present more resembles hell as it was depicted in the premodern era.

But unlike the people of the premodern era, we can no longer resort to the protection of myth and religion that has the power of revealed truth -- be it the truth about ourselves or about the world at large. Past traditions tell us that only people with good heart and pure intentions can safely cross the border into the realm of the unknown. But our culture is no longer equipped with the means to create "good people" in the traditional sense, because we left behind those means when we entered modern technological society.

I doubt that an attempt to change the course by trying to reestablish old values could succeed at this point, because the foundations of humanistic traditions are so terribly eroded. I can therefore sympathize with the seventy-nine-year-old H.G. Wells who, at the ebb of his life, felt that:

> The world is at the end of its tether. The end of everything we call life is close at hand and cannot be evaded.... Our universe is not merely bankrupt, there remains no dividend at all; it has not simply liquidated; it is going clean out of existence, leaving not a wrack behind. The attempt to trace a pattern of any sort is absolutely futile.

> Homo Sapiens, as he has been pleased to call himself, is in his present form played out. The stars in their course have turned against him and he has to give place to some other animal better adapted to face the fate that closes on more and more swiftly upon mankind. That new animal may be an entirely alien strain, or it may arise as a new modification of the hominidae, and even a direct continuation of the human phylum, but it will certainly not be human. [4]

NOTES

1. For a more elaborate discussion on this point see: George Steiner, In Bluebeard's Castle, London: Faber & Faber, 1971, pp. 65-70.

2. Steiner, In Bluebeard's Castle, p. 23

3. Heinrich Heine, History of Religion and Philosophy in Germany in the Prose Writings of Heinrich Heine, ed. & trans. Havelock Ellis, London, 1887.

4. H.G. Wells, Mind at the End of its Tether, N.Y.: Didier, 1946, pp. 1, 17, 18, 19.

MODERNITY AND RELIGIOUS STUDIES
K. Dad Prithipaul

Every now and then some concerned scholar engaged in the study of religious phenomena comes up with an appraisal of what has been achieved by the departments of religion. Within the university set up this ritual takes place once every decade or so. For the present purpose, I refer to the article by Professor Walter H. Capps in the October 1981 issue of the Bulletin of the Council on the Study of Religion (vol. 12, no. 4). He raises the question of how the student of religion has to confront the universal with the quotidian. Reinhold Niebuhr, he says, used to remind his students that it was indispensable for them to read the Holy Bible and The New York Times. While not seeking the instant joys of relevance, Capps argues for a recognition of the fact that -- whether we like it or not -- religion still remains at the heart of the burning issues of the times. Referring to recent events, he raises the problem of the failure of religion specialists to understand the up-heaval in Iran, the conflict in Ireland, or the tragedy of Jonestown. At the centre of this failure to understand these varied, but kindred, phenomena is the impoverishment of the discipline of religious studies. He recalls that religious studies departments came into being largely because they held out the promise of filling the void left by, in par-ticular, the departments of philosophy which abdicated their existential responsibilities and of departments of psychology which surrendered to the allure of behaviourism. Into this empty space the department of religious studies was expected to erect a structure within which all the moral and spiritual preoccupations of modern man were to manifest themselves:

> The implication is that religious studies gained insti-tutional support when it had also earned moral sup-port. It had moral support because it had a larger collective respect. It was understood to make sense given the intellectual questions -- yes, the human agenda -- of the time. [1]

The departments of religious studies went awry or failed to make any decisive impact on the intellectual life of the continent when they chose to restrict themselves almost exclusively to an examination of

data related to the past. The programs have had little to say about the
present and practically nothing about the future. Religion does indeed
remain the indispensable focus of any true understanding of the past
history of the classical civilizations, certainly of the civilizations
in which we are all involved. One of the signs of the failure -- within
the institution -- of the religion programs is the persistent suspicion
with which academics working in other disciplines consider anything that
is related, however remotely, to the religious. We still have to
contend with the pervasive opinion, still very much part of contemporary
enlightened rationality, that associates obscurantism, conflict, and
backwardness with all forms of religiosity. The same enlightened
rationality takes for granted the fact that the men of the classics
spent their time burning each other's cities, or that the atheistic
ideologies have proved in the twentieth century to be more destructive
of human lives and of the aesthetic and intellectual achievements of
generations of artists and thinkers. The reason for this suspicion of
the religions is to be sought not only in the disinterestedness of the
dilettante or in the pride or self-sufficiency of the non-believing
academic or politician.

The reason for the suspicion with which our endeavours are beheld
is to be sought rather in the refusal, on the part of the academic, to
understand and respond intelligently to the meaningfulness of our enterprise; especially in the humanities where one-track mindedness is exten-
sively cultivated. This insensitivity is further sustained by an environment in which the elites have consciously eliminated almost completely the need for mythic thinking and the maintenance of symbols
related to the transcendent. Our work is consequently restricted by the
inability of the educated public to perceive the purposefulness of the
teaching of the religions. The emphasis higher education has placed on
over-specialization, by the institutionalization of the division of
labour ushered in by the Industrial Revolution in the West,[2] has resulted in the development of an educated public fragmented into a
congeries of mutually exclusive intellectual tastes and preoccupations.
We do not have a broad literate audience where each member, while
pursuing a specific professional avocation, would at the same time be
cognizant of the relevance of the sublime and the poetic in daily life.

Capps does indeed recognize that

> religious studies must always carry a double focus:
> first, on what counts as 'hard data', or on the sub-

jects to which the specific inquiry is directed; and second a kind of sophisticated self-consciousness about the larger frameworks, interest and attention under whose auspices the inquiry is being carried out. In short, religious studies deals not simply with the data, but also with the process by which the data are translated into human knowledge. [3]

Capps' analysis of the problem is timely and pertinent. It is important that we recognize that our program is becoming increasingly irrelevant and sterile. As he points out:

Perhaps it is because the data have been uncovered at too rapid a pace and it is nearly impossible to keep up with all of it. But it seems that we have given too little attention to the comprehensive grasp, that is, to the ways in which what has been uncovered affects our general theories about religion. Instead we are opting for a preoccupation with matters much more regional, specific and parochical. And the sign that something is lacking is our propensity to look outside our own field for theories of comprehensive generalizations. [4]

The inadequacy of the program of religious studies stems from the fact that we do not seem to realize -- or, if we do, we fail to bring this awareness into the framework of our intellectual preoccupations -- that there exists, according to the Indian tradition, two forms of the validity of knowledge. One type of knowledge has intrinsic validity and the other has extrinsic validity. The knowledge that acquires intrinsic validity is that knowledge which blends itself into an ongoing tradition. Its characteristic is Truth -- permanent, eternal. The other type of knowledge has only a provisional relevance. It is used by some, benefits a few, and is rejected by others. It is discarded as time passes. In the departments of religious studies we are, for the most part, engaged in the acquisition and dissemination of knowledge that has only extrinsic validity. There is little common measure, for instance, between the substance of our work and publications and the enterprise of the scholastic doctors whose writings and preachings for centuries helped mould the minds and consciences, the passions and the hopes, of believers. Their insights and their devotions lent themselves to achievements well beyond the narrow confines of book learning. During those long periods, their writings and teachings had ramifications in the art, the legal institutions, the political ideologies, and the economic structures that held the social hierarchies together. The literary productions of the religious studies programs have yielded practically no viable body of ideas and norms that have gone to enrich the living traditions. No art form, no myth has been generated by the scientific study of religions. Yet, while some mysterious urge seems to maintain the vitality of the living faiths like some secret life-giving sap in a tree whose growth remains invisible to the eye, our program remains external to this process of persistence and growth in the different religions of the world. We have placed our pursuits under the aegis of scientific rigour and our understanding is at best a reminder that our intellectual work does not affect the substance and the dynamism of the religions which project their traditions well into the future. Still we are left with no alternative to the consideration of the religious "fact" as the object of our study, on the understanding that the religious fact is not to be viewed as a thing. It is always a person, a believer. The human being is metaphysics alive as history.

COMPARATIVE RELIGION

The inadequacies of religious studies concomitantly reflect the impotence of the comparative study of religion in its ability to rise above the status of academic dilettantism. For more than a century, since it came into being as a by-product of Western imperialism, the comparison of religion has not brought about an effective and lasting understanding on the part of one believer of the religion of another. The findings of those who have endeavoured to compare one religion with another have been studied only by the specialists. They have not effected any change in the social consciousness of the adherents of one religion with regard to their perception of the other religion or culture. In particular, the religion departments have made no attempt to understand that the

> Renaissance, which is not only a cultural movement,
> but the twin birth of capitalism and colonialism, far
> from being the culmination of humanism, has destroyed
> civilizations superior to that of the West, regarding

the relationships between Man and Nature, society and the divine.[5]

The creation of an authentic future requires that we rediscover all the dimensions of Man developed in the non-Western civilizations and cultures.[6]

That each of us belongs to a religion which, in a global context, is a minority, ought to prompt us to understand the limitations of our endeavour. Above all, we must remind ourselves that

this manner, on the part of the Western man, to consider that the individual is the measure of all
things, to reduce all reality to the concept, that is,
to treat science as a supreme value and the techniques
as a means to manipulate things and men, is a minute
exception in the human epic of three million years.[7]

Comparative religion grew out of the nineteenth-century curiosity, on the part of some Western philologists and philosophers, about the beliefs and practices of the peoples which belonged to the non-Christian religions. Those who embarked on this luxury academic exercise were little aware of the drift that had already started well into the six-teenth century with the dawn of the Enlightenment and its celebration of reason. The comparative study of religion was undertaken with the enthusiasm generated by the widespread belief in progress, particularly in the business of understanding cultures with which the West had had little acquaintance. It was an offshoot of the scientism which, as the repository of certainty, was then inexorably displacing traditional religion with its requirement of faith. It has had no social impact. Beyond the superficial aesthetic interest shown by the Romantics in the spiritual writings of the Orientals, the impact never reached below the surface of Western consciousness.

This will remain so for generations to come. This need not be viewed as a statement of pessimism, or of despair. First of all there is no need for anyone to understand the religion of the other, for the simple reason that an academic obligation is not to be confused with a cultural necessity, or with a moral need. Decades of study of the world religions and of the experience of teaching oriental thought in the West have now convinced me that a specific structure of knowledge, of a

theological nature, acts as an opaque screen which prevents any purpose-
ful grasp of the values enshrined in a different religious tradition.
The distance between fidelity to one's own tradition and a right existential acceptance of what the other professes remains and will remain
infinite. On the other hand, structures of prejudice and of misunderstanding have become more immediately part of the quotidian.

For the purpose of this discussion I shall isolate two notions,
among others, which to my mind lie at the root of the inability of the
believer within the Judaeo-Christian tradition to fully comprehend the
substance of the oriental religions. I refer to the notions of Nature
and Error. Beginning with the ancients, Western man has produced an
impressive literature on Nature. The persistent strain of thought that
has run through all the formulations of what Nature is, is the externality of Man with regard to it. The duality of Man and Nature is
inherent in the foundational tenets of the Judaeo-Christian complex of
religions. On the other hand, in the Hindu, Buddhist, and Taoist
religions, Man knows Nature as himself. Man is part of Nature, he is in
Nature and he is Nature. The two metaphysical presuppositions are
diametrically opposed to each other.

The notion that Nature must be conquered and used to favour Man's
needs is essentially Western. The desire to conquer Nature, to unlock
its mysteries, becomes the central preoccupation of Western man, beginning with Bacon, Newton, and the sciences fostered by the reaffirmation
of reason in the era of the Enlightenment. Little did Western man
anticipate that the celebration of reason would culminate in the twentieth century with a horror of inhumanity, perpetrated on a scale that
still defies the imagination. In his courageous analysis of the metaphysical and religious antecedents of the bureaucratic thought which
made Auschwitz a historical reality, Richard Rubenstein brings out the
underlying affinities which link the processes of secularization, disenchantment, and rationalization. [8] The author of the Book of Genesis
testifies to a world devoid of mysterious forces where man can do whatever he pleases as long as he is at peace with the extra-terrestrial
creator. Adam is asked to "subdue" the earth and to exert dominion over
it (Genesis 1:28).

The biblical attitude that nature is devoid of divine and magic
powers is extended to the political order. The secularization process
originates in the Bible. There is a difference between the Biblical
notion of political order and the modern notion. In the biblical world,
man lives in the knowledge of the judgement of a righteous, omnipotent

deity. But, for all practical purposes, the righteous and omnipotent divinity has disappeared from the political consciousness of modern man. An attempt at re-enchanting the world is made by Roman Catholicism with its emphasis on God's presence in the saints or in sacred times and places, while vigorously maintaining the distinction between a super-natural world of divinity and a world devoid of mysterious and magical powers. By its affirmation that man is saved only by faith, not by works, Protestantism rejects this attempt by Roman Catholicism to re-enchant the created order. Protestantism thus separates man's actions in this world from the divine realm with a logic that had been initiated by biblical Judaism but which it could not attain.

It was thus no coincidence that it is the land of Reformation which first perfected bureaucracy in its objective form and where such a bureaucracy could produce its completely secularized, rationalized, and dehumanized "achievement" -- the death camp. Rubenstein persuasively asserts that the secularization process is not antithetical to religiosity. On the contrary, it is biblical Judaism which initiates this process when it frees significant areas of human activity from religious domination and ushers in a movement that inevitably leads to what is simply called "modern paganism." Rubenstein warns us against the mistake of returning to the Judaeo-Christian values without properly distinguishing between the manifest values a tradition holds to be binding and the ethos which it subsequently generates. The Judaeo-Christian tradition proclaims every creature to be made in the image of God, yet it has unintentionally produced a secularization of consciousness and a consequent dehumanized rationality which has, for all practical purposes, almost totally eliminated any sentiment of respect for human dignity. In contrast to the humanism of the Greco-Roman traditions, it is the Judaeo-Christian tradition which has brought about the secularization of consciousness, the disenchantment of the world, and methodical conduct and bureaucratic objectivity.[9]

The institutionalization of care for objectivity and method has ushered in a withering of the psyche which has become a banal part of the present human condition. The religion of the churches has contributed not a little to the reduction of the vision of the transcendent. It becomes difficult to reconcile oneself to the inexorable progress of a rationality that during the last so many centuries has succeeded in drying up the well from which sprang all that is vital in the religious sensitivity. The result is that today we are at a loss as to how to restore the mystical vision to the individual and the collective consciousness.

> The repression of the religious sensibilities in our
> culture over the past few centuries has been as much
> an adjunct of social and economic necessity as any act
> of class oppression or physical exploitation. [10]

More than three centuries of a triumphant rationality which has shrunk the scope of our sensitivity to the transcendent and mysterious in the world around us have landed us in a psychic wasteland; the ecological blight outside is but a mirror of what is inside. Our faith in and reliance on industrialization have obliterated from our metaphysical economy the memory and index of our first principle. We are bonded in allegiance to Urizen, Blake's demon of Reason and Technical Power, in his remorseless desire to vegetate the divine vision. [11]

> In the industrial west, we remain heavily saddled with
> capitalist business and politics as usual, if lately
> mellowed and grown highly sophisticated in its public
> relations. But our culture, while dominated by
> science-based industrialism, has been in revolutionary
> ferment since the industrial economy first began to
> devour the landscape. The origin of this ferment lies
> in that tempestuous artistic outburst we call the
> Romantic movement. From it, we inherit a stubborn
> counter-cultural resistance to the pre-eminence of
> science, to its technological elaborations and to its
> manifold imitators in the humanities, arts, and so-
> called behavioral sciences.
> Significant that this rebellious opposition
> consciousness should have emerged most vividly in the
> arts -- and should have largely remained there, giving
> us our singular tradition of the artist as outlaw,
> rebel, lunatic, misfit, rogue. Why should this be?
> Perhaps because the burden of alienation weighs most
> heavily on the creative powers; because the beauties
> of science are not the beauties of art but their an-
> tithesis. Who recognizes a cage for what it is? Not
> canaries of careful Reason who value well-fortified

shelter but skylarks whose song needs the space and
sunlight beyond the bars. And what does it tell us
about the nature of our religious tradition in the
west that it should be the arts and not the churches
that have produced far and away the greater number of
modern martyrs, persecuted prophets, and suffering
saints? [12]

During the past decades, poets, artists, and even psychologists
have been alerting us about the tragic consequences of man's use of
techniques of domination while being stricken with a fragmented psyche.
The spectacular reservoir of knowledge which Western man has accumulated
still leaves him in utter ignorance of his own psyche. [13]

Through his historical development, the European has
become so far removed from his roots that his mind was
finally split into faith and knowledge, in the same
way that every psychological exaggeration breaks up
into its inherent opposites. He needs to return, not
to Nature in the manner of Rousseau, but to his own
nature. His task is to find the natural man again.
Instead of this, there is nothing he likes better than
systems and methods by which he can repress the
natural man who is everywhere at cross purposes with
him. He will infallibly make a wrong use of yoga
because his psychic disposition is quite different
from that of the Oriental. I say to whomsoever I can:
"Study yoga -- you will learn an infinite amount from
it -- but do not try to apply it, for we Europeans are
not so constituted that we apply these methods correctly, just like that. An Indian guru can explain
everything and you can imitate everything. But do you
know who is applying the yoga? In other words, do you
know who you are and how you are constituted?" [14]

Jung, however, adheres to a sort of intuitive optimism rooted in
his faith that, intellectual ignorance notwithstanding, the psyche is
"there" within us. He hopes for a future when Western man will finally
reach home and come to rest in the assurance of self-knowledge. He
believes that this can be accomplished by rescuing what in Christianity

is valid for this purpose.

> Western man has no need of more superiority over
> nature, whether outside or inside. He has both in
> almost devilish perfection. What he lacks is con-
> scious recognition of his inferiority to the nature
> around and within him. He must learn that he may not
> do exactly as he wills. If he does not learn this,
> his own nature will destroy him. He does not know
> that his own soul is rebelling against him in a
> suicidal way.... But since one cannot detach oneself
> from something of which one is unconscious, the
> European must first learn to know his subject. This,
> in the West, is what one calls the unconscious. Yoga
> technique applies itself exclusively to the conscious
> mind and will.... When the yogi says "prana" he means
> very much more than mere breath. For him the word
> prana brings with it the full weight of its metaphysi-
> cal components, and it is as if he really knew what
> prana meant in this respect. He does not know it with
> his understanding, but with his heart, belly, and
> blood. The European only imitates and learns ideas by
> rote, and is therefore incapable of expressing his
> subjective facts through Indian concepts. [15]

He also says:

> For me the unconscious is a collective psychic dis-
> position, creative in character.... But no insight is
> gained by repressing and controlling the unconscious,
> and least of all by imitating methods which have grown
> up under totally different psychological conditions.
> In the course of the centuries the West will produce
> its own yoga, and it will be on the basis laid down by
> Christianity. [16]

THE EASTERN VIEW

In contrast to Western man, the Hindu or the Buddhist knows Nature
in his own self. His apprehension of matter coincides with his study of
that body. He perceives Nature in it, and it becomes a space where the

distinction between the outside and the inside is abolished. The sentiment of the identity with the totality of Nature leads inevitably to the
need for a clear grasp of his own inner nature, his true self. The
unitiveness of the cosmos corresponds to the sentiment of the homogene-
ousness of the ultimate reality and his Self. Thus the Indian perceives
his oneness with Being, both in the cosmic manifestation and in the
manifestation of which he is the place. He takes for granted the
reality of the psyche, hidden from his existential preoccupation in his
care for empirical expectations of achievement and failure.

That the Indian would find it natural to invent and develop a
technique for self-realization is thus not due to accident. It proceeds
from a particular mindfulness and an attentiveness to the ultimate
pervasive reality. Being is co-existent with phenomenal existence. His
concern is to attune himself to a hearing of Being. He then proceeds to
a reflection on Being. In the last stage he contemplates Being. He
finally discovers that there is no distinction between himself and
Brahman, or the Buddha Nature. All that matters therefore is to sustain
relentlessly his care for Being. At the same time the chasm between the
Western theological and the Oriental philosophical attitude remains
impossible to bridge. Jung says:

> In the East, where these ideas and practices origin-
> ated and where an uninterrrupted tradition extending
> over some four thousand years has created the neces-
> sary spiritual conditions, yoga is, as I can readily
> believe, the perfect and appropriate method of fusing
> body and mind together so that they form a unity that
> can hardly be doubted. Thus they create a psychologi-
> cal disposition which makes possible intuitions that
> transcend consciousness. The Indian mentality has no
> difficulty in operating intelligently with a concept
> like prana. The West, on the contrary, with its bad
> habit of wanting to believe on the one hand, and its
> highly developed scientific and philosophical critique
> on the other, finds itself in a real dilemma. Either
> it falls into the trap of faith and swallows concepts
> like prajna, atman, chakra, samadhi etc. without
> giving them a thought, or its scientific critique
> repudiates them one and all as "pure mysticism." The
> split in the Western mind therefore makes it impos-

> sible at the outset for the intentions of yoga to be
> realized in any adequate way.... The Indian can forget
> neither the mind nor the body, while the European is
> always forgetting either the one or the other. With
> this capacity to forget he has, for the time being,
> conquered the world. Not so the Indian. He not only
> knows his own nature, but he knows how much he himself
> is nature. The European, on the other hand, has a
> science of nature and knows astonishingly little of
> his own nature, the nature within him.... [17]

This split translates itself into a forgetting of the unconscious and of
the psyche.

Written in 1933, these lines of Jung have lost none of their relevance. In those days they might have struck one as being pessimistic.
Today one wonders why so little attention has been paid to them. With
some poignancy he exposes, in psychological and medical terms, the chasm
which separates the Western from the Oriental preoccupations with the
discovering of Being. I am not arguing that the chasm must be viewed as
a negative value in itself. Nor am I contemplating the divergence
between the two views of the world and of man as being necessarily un-
desirable. I am striving to establish the stark reality of the anthropological plurality that undergirds the fundamentals of the classical
religions. Jung arrives at his conclusions on empirical, clinical
grounds.

It is edifying to recognize the confirmation of Jung's Western
views of the psyche in a "liberal" theologian's analysis of Christian
traditions, and the difference between the fundamental religious attitudes professed by the Christian and the Hindu. Hans Küng condemns as
dogmatic the religion which, in Ancient Greece and later in the Enlightenment, rejects myth as a prescientific form of knowledge and erects
rational "scientific" knowledge into an absolute subordinating everything religious to it. [18] He finds a similarity between this "rational"
rejection of myth and S. Radhakrishnan's view that all religions in
their rites and symbols, teachings and languages, are actually manifestations of the same underlying mystical reality. This inner spiritual
experience is the only absolute reality. Küng qualifies this view as
dogmatic because it leaves out Christ. Küng -- wrongly -- argues that
experience of identity is contrary to revelation. Obedience to the
Willing God is a higher order of religious experience than absorption

into the ultimate reality.[19]

It is pertinent to observe here that, like the early Greeks, the Hindu and Buddhist do not have a word for "will," in the sense in which it is used in the spiritual literature of the West. Maurice Blondel's L'Action and Paul Ricoeur's Philosophie de la Volonté magnificently hypostasize the logic of moral action within a religious ideology of obedience and of fidelity to an extra-natural deity. On the other hand, both Hinduism and Buddhism attribute to moral action the negative function of ending the separation of the self from the ultimate reality. In one view the ultimate experience is the pure act which seeks for and strives to produce a harmony of knowing, of willing, and of being.[20] The supreme triumph of the will is our submission which enables us to acquire God. Action is the only receptacle that can hold the divine gift, it is the necessary condition for faith to serve as a passage between the Will and the Supreme Being which is ever present and active in all things. To will is to will to be, but in collaboration with Being. To will to be without Being is to lose oneself.[21] In contrast the Hindu-Buddhist view postulates action which strives to annihilate itself: to act is to be. Becoming is the allurement, it is not reality. Action does not effect any change: it is the unveiling of Being and its identity with Existence. It is the locus where Being enters Time.

If the mystical vision considered as the ultimate religious experience does not muster the adherence of even a "liberal" theologian like Küng, and there is no compelling reason why he should not hold to his convictions, then we are left with no other choice but to conclude that, however absurd it may appear, Man has invented a plurality of metaphysical universes of which histories and civilizations are their temporal and spatial symbols. Cicero was wrong to say that "No single thing is so like one another, so exactly its counterpart, as all of us are to one another."[22]

We do therefore concur with Kipling's decisive conclusion that the twain shall never meet. Western man sees his destiny welded to a linear unfolding of Truth in History. The Hindu prefers to see himself in a spherical, immediate identity between the microcosm and the macrocosm. If History is the unfolding of the truth, the revealed truth, Küng would like to Procrusteanize the history of all mankind to conform to the norms of Western history. For the Indian then, the problem — if it is a problem — can only be solved by ignoring it and walling himself up within a blinkered perception of his own tradition.

This approach of mutual exclusiveness dominates the scene within the programs of religious studies. Loyalty to the linear development of history does not foster the intellectual hospitality towards categories of thinking and of feeling, borrowed from other traditions, which could be used to explain, justify, or integrate truth postulates as handed down within the Western tradition. All of us remain bound to our geography, both physical and mental. Dogmatic theological exclusivism bears no correspondence to the present historical landscape where the human race lives materially, at every moment, a single process of mutual dependence on a universal scale.

ANTHROPOLOGY

The divergent views of nature and of history are reflected in equally divergent anthropological definitions. For the sake of clarity we shall compare the anthropology of the Indian with that of the Jahvist. The Mandukya Upanishad gives a lucid analysis of the different psychic states as those of wakefulness, dream, and deep sleep. These are the manifestations of Turiya, the fourth state. The Turiya is the absolute self. Knowledge of the Turiya is the ultimate experience. It is also an experience which abolishes all mental constructions. It is a knowledge which follows, not precedes, faith. Gnosis is thus a meta-perception. Beyond it there is no other object, however sublime, to be seen. The self is both the seer and the seen. It is the prover and the proved. The Buddhist further explains it with dramatic simplicity: one becomes awakened, by oneself, without the help of an external agent.

The ultimate in Man for the Jahvist is not the direct identity with Being. It is an attribute. It is goodness, it is innocence. The imago dei is simultaneously being-created and innocence. The "goodness" of creation is nothing else than its status as creature. A creation is good and the goodness specific to man is to be the image of God. Seen retrospectively from the moment of sin as a prior state, in the mythic language, this resemblance appears as a lack of culpability, as inno-cence. But its goodness is quite positive, it is sin that is the nothingness of vanity. Thus can one interpret the states of innocence and of sin, not in succession, but in super-imposition. Sin does not follow innocence, but in the instant loses it. In the instant I am born, in the same instant I fall. I am created in the instant: actual-ly my pristine goodness is my status of being-created. But I never cease being-created, under penalty to be. Consequently I do not cease being good. Henceforth, the "event" of the sin terminates the innocence in the instant; it is, in the instant, the discontinuity, the fracture, of my being-created and of my becoming bad. The myth brings into succession what is simultaneous and cannot not be so. It brings to an end a "prior" state of innocence in an instant which begins the posterior state of curse. But this is how it reaches its depth: by relating the fall as an event, sprung from one does not know where, it gives to anthropology a key concept: the contingency of this radical evil which the penitent is always on the verge of calling his "bad nature." Thus the myth denounces the purely historical characteristic of this radical evil.

In his analysis of the adamic myth, Paul Ricoeur establishes the difference that lies at the root of the problem which we are contemplating.[23] For Sankara, God or Being is neither an attribute, nor a relationship, nor a species. It requires the mediacy of nothing. It is pure contemplation, it is psychic expression. It is, psychologically speaking, nirvikalpa-samadhi. It has no form, no name. On the other hand, the pure man, the innocent Adam, is a creature, distinct from Being and from God. Sin, or "fallen-ness," is external, it is accidental; it is not his true essence, which is innocence. The ultimate essence, if we may use this term, of Adam is a quality which sets him apart from the Creator. The duality between Adam and God is fundamental. The harmony between God and Adam is established by obedience, by fulfilment of the commandments in a linear historical process. The Hindu takes an immediate view of his relation to the Absolute Being, on the model of what goes on in his mind. The thought process does indeed happen in a serial sequence, but not in a straight line. Indeed, thought never experiences the straight line. For the Hindu, the thought process is chaos. Order is nothing less than the disappearance of chaos, of the thought process itself, when the transrational reality is reached. Chaos is error, it is psychic error. Error is not inscribed in the cosmos or in Nature, it is man's nature. Error is consequently an inherent component of the Mind, the result of the afflictions that already exist in it. Attentiveness to Being therefore consists of the negation of the psychological afflictions which are external to the Self. The technique of the recovery of one's nature is a technique of negation. The neti, neti is the cognitive expression of this negative act of removing what is a superfluous accretion on Being. The inauthentic Self in its empirical activities is superimposed on Being. Once this imposition is removed, Being shines forth in all its lustre.

IMMANENCE

Such a hypostasis is admissible on the assumption that Being, or God, is immanent. At the same time -- if reconciliation be a necessity -- this appears as a stumbling block. The Western theologian cannot accept the fact that the transcendent can be encountered in the temporal process. For the Hindu, God is Eternity -- he is also Time. [24] The Suttavibhanga tells the following beautiful parable:

> When a hen has laid eggs, says the Buddha, eight or ten or twelve of them, and she has sat upon them and kept them warm for a sufficient time; and when the first chick breaks through the shell with his toe or beak and issues happily from the egg, what shall we call this chick, the oldest or the youngest? -- We shall call him the oldest, venerable Gautama, for he is the first born among them -- So likewise, O Brahman, I alone among men who live in ignorance and are as though enclosed and imprisoned in an egg have burst this shell of ignorance, and I alone in all the world have obtained the beatific universal dignity of the Buddha. Thus, O Brahman, I am the oldest, the noblest among men. [25]

ERROR

Error is the other notion that impedes cross-fertilization between the different religions. We may again refer to Hans Küng's view about non-Christian world religions:

> The world religions do, though in error, proclaim God's truth. Though they are far from God, God is not far from them. Though they flee from the true God, they are yet graciously held on to by him who is also their God. By him they are made able, in the midst of all their errors, to speak truly of him....
>
> As against the "extraordinary" way of salvation which is the Church, the world religions can be called -- if this is rightly understood -- the "ordinary" way of salvation for non-Christian humanity. God is the Lord not only of the special salvation history of the

Church, but also of the universal salvation history of
all mankind; this universal salvation history is bound
up with the special salvation history in having a
common origin, meaning and goal and being subject to
the same grace of God. Every historical situation,
outside the Church as well as inside it, is thus
included in advance within his grace. Since God
seriously and effectively wills that all men should be
saved and that none should be lost unless by his own
fault, every man is intended to find his salvation
within his own historical condition.... The religions
with their forms of belief and cult, their categories
and values, their symbols and ordinances, their
religious and ethical experience, thus have a "relative validity."[26]

For his part, the Indian views error as arising from a double
source. In his natural condition, he understands his separation from
Being as cosmic ignorance. In a private sense this metaphysical ignorance is known psychologically as the afflictions of the mind. Truth
then is not an effect realized by action. It is the negation of ignorance. It is an experience of the Self by the Self. It takes place
within the existential process. It is self-validated.

In following its interests, Reason knows its limitations and
strives to lead the self beyond it by means of an imaginative leap
through faith. For the Hindu, faith is related to a mythic image.
Freedom consists first in the construction of a visual image of a
personal divinity which, by means of a symbolic philanthropy, constantly
mirrors the presence of the Godhead. His care for Being is fulfilled in
the instant by a free mythic projection. Being is outside, because it
is within. Being is sought because it is already our essence, our
substance. The Indian understands Pascal to whom Brahman would say:
"You would not seek me if you did not already know me to be you." Faith
for the Indian serves as a subsidiary to knowledge. Transcendent Being
is prior to existence. Faith then ushers the existent to a direct
acquaintance with Being. The spatial attribute of the externality of
Being is at best a mode of speaking to oneself. Speech is here directed
to one's self. It becomes the Self. It is silence. Being reveals
itself: it is not an attribute, it is not a relation, it is not a
species. It is the ground of myself; it is myself.

The Indian view thus succeeds, in its linguistic articulations, its method and techniques of investigation, in unveiling Being within the existential process. What seems paradoxical to the Oriental is the persistence in the Western tradition of the unwillingness to take the leap away from the metaphysics of obedience into the experience of identity. What appears tragic to the Oriental is that the primacy of Reason in the West has succeeded in preventing Western man from postulating Being-Knowledge as the centrality of his metaphysical and

Plato thought it was impossible to translate the possibility of the naturally good into actual knowledge.[27] With Hegel the distinction between the actual and the rational was abolished. The problem after Hegel became the epilogical transformation of the thoughtful triumph of Enlightenment into a worldly triumph.[28]

> What Diderot, Kant, Hegel and Marx shared was a
> certainty that reason could dispel myth and that to do
> so was desirable. To each, the root of evil was man's
> ignorance of the world. The world would yield its
> theoretical and sensual bounties if only one could
> finally grasp its principles. Between this end and
> man stood the intellectual format of man's darkness --
> myth. It was myth that kept science from probing the
> nature of the world. But science possessed its own
> power: by its nature, science progressively dispelled
> myth. As reason and science triumphed, the historical
> millenium would be ushered in.[29]

While theology in the West could never appreciate the spiritual categories at work in the living traditions with which it came into contact, it also failed to subsume the drift initiated with the proclamation by the Greek philosophers of Reason as the highest manifestation of humanity. Theology yielded to the spirit of self-sufficiency and of progress ushered in by the thinkers, artists, and scientists of the Enlightenment. Myth was banished as an impediment to knowledge. All darkness was believed to be dispelled: it was enough to grasp the principles and theories, and the earth would open its secrets to inquiring reason. The warnings of Rousseau went unheeded. He wrote:

> Peoples, know once and for all that nature wanted to
> keep you from being harmed by knowledge just as a

mother wrests a dangerous weapon from her child's hands, that all the secrets she hides from you are so many evils from which she protects you. [30]

Theology could not sense that the trust in Reason alone would land mankind in the horrors that have marked this century. Strangely enough, those who were most keenly aware of the tragic denouement of the Enlightenment were not theologians, but poets like Blake and Goethe. They were political figures like Mahatma Gandhi and psychological and medical scientists like Jung. They were sociologists such as those who formed the Frankfurt School. What is baffling is that despite these enormous tragedies, the institutions of higher learning -- in particular the universities -- do not appear to have been touched with a sense of tragedy. The drift continues.

CONCLUSION

I was indeed surprised to learn that this conference was to be organized around the concept of modernity. It was surprising because one would surmise that more than five centuries after Petrarch we would not still be questioning the implications of modernity. For the purpose of my argument I shall use Jung's definition of modernity. He says:

Every good quality has its bad side, and nothing that is good can come into the world without directly producing a corresponding evil. This is a painful fact. Now there is the danger that consciousness of the present may lead to an elation based upon illusion: the illusion, namely, that we are the culmination of the history of mankind, the fulfilment and the end-product of countless centuries. If we grant this, we should understand that it is no more than the proud acknowledgement of our destitution: we are also the disappointment of the hopes and expectations of the ages. Think of nearly two thousand years of Christian ideals followed, instead of by the return of the Messiah and the heavenly millenium, by the World War among Christian nations and its barbed-wire and poison-gas. What a catastrophe in heaven and on earth!

In the face of such a picture we may well grow humble again. It is true that modern man is a culmination, but tomorrow he will be surpassed; he is indeed the end-product of an age-old development, but he is at the same time the worst conceivable disappointment of the hopes of humankind. The modern man is aware of this. He has seen how beneficent are science, technology and organization, but also how catastrophic they can be. He has likewise seen that well-meaning governments have so thoroughly paved the way for peace on the principle "in time of peace prepare for war," that Europe has nearly gone to rack and ruin. As for ideals, the Christian church, the brotherhood of man, international social democracy and the "solidarity" of economic interests have all failed to stand the baptism of fire -- the test of reality. Today, fifteen years after the war, we observe once more the same optimism, the same organization, the same political aspirations, the same phrases and catch-words at work. How can we but fear that they will inevitably lead to further catastrophes? Agreements to outlaw war leave us sceptical, even while we wish them all possible success. At bottom, behind every such palliative measure, there is a gnawing doubt. On the whole, I believe I am not exaggerating when I say that modern man has suffered an almost fatal shock, psychologically speaking, and as a result has fallen into profound uncertainty.[31]

These words sound particularly pathetic when we recall that they were written only six years before the Second World War broke out.

We continue to live as herd-beings, without the things of the spirit. The psychology which informs our culture and our academic pursuits is not based on the established structures of faith or myth or of philosophical insights. We are in conflict with ourselves, buffeted by the wild reaches of change that leave us bewildered, without moorings.

In our programs, we in religious studies do not bear in mind that a culture has a day-side and a night-side. We do not know how to translate in one comprehensive grasp the totality of a religion, the totality of the culture it founds, or the totality of human experience. We do not serve -- to use Heidegger's felicitous expression -- as the "Shepherds of Being." Our essential failure lies in our inability to construct a corpus of valid knowledge that can provide to the totality of the student the symbols and the means of integrating Being in Existence. What is worse, we have not been able to do that even on an aesthetic level.

Why should the student of religion be concerned with modernity? What is the relationship between Being and modernity? Modernity is vanity. It is not an attribute of Being. If we are here to grapple with the issues raised by modernity, we must have the courage to admit that we are lost. At best, we do not know where we are going.

At every moment of history, men and women have seen themselves as witnesses to a modern age. It is a recurrent attitude of nostalgia for every generation to look up to a previous period as having been richer, more compassionate, and offering more opportunities for self-fulfillment. In recent years, social scientists, mainly in the West, have fashioned the notion of modernity to equip a methodology required for a logical explanation of certain clusters of social phenomena. Modernity is not an entity in itself; it is not a new knowledge. It is not a metaphysical reality. It is not even a style.

The new scale of warfare, the shifts of economic forces, the pervasiveness of techniques in individual and corporate existence, the explosion of knowledge and the mushrooming of populations -- these and other historical developments may bring about a numbed obliviousness with regard to the reality of the visionary experience. But, on that account, this reality does not cease to be.

The study of religion may take note of the peripheral relevance of modernity jargon while the fundamentals of religion have little -- if anything -- to do with it. Indeed, whatever we do ought not to be in terms of a why and a wherefore:

> Now I will give you my opinion about what it means to
> be a human. Homo is the same thing here as a human
> being to whom a substance has been given, and this
> gives a human being existence and life, and it is an
> existence endowed with reason. The truly reasonable
> human beings are those who understand themselves with
> their reason and then free themselves from all materi-
> al things as well as forms. The more people are free

of all things and turn to themselves, the more they
will know in themselves all things clearly with their
reason, without any hindrance from outside. And the
more they do this, the more they are truly human.[32]

And again:

the just person does not seek anything with his work,
for every single person who seeks anything or even
something with his or her works is working for a why
and is a servant and a mercenary. Therefore, if you
wish to be conformed and transformed into justice, do
not intend anything in your work and strive for no
why, either in time or in eternity. Do not aim at
reward or blessedness, neither this nor that....
Therefore, if you want to live and if you want your
works to live, you must be dead to all things and you
must become in touch with nothingness. It is peculiar
to the creature that it makes something from something; but it is peculiar to God to make something
from nothing. Therefore, for God to make something in
you or with you, you must first make contact with this
nothingness. Therefore, enter into your own ground
and work there and these works which you work there
will all be living. And therefore the wise person
says: "The just person lives." For because he is
just, he works and his works live.[33]

Scripture says: "Before the creation of the world, I
am" (Si. 24:9). This means "Before I am" which means
that if a person is raised up beyond time into
eternity, then the person works one work there with
God. Some people ask how a person can work these
works which God has worked a thousand years ago and
which God will work a thousand years from now and they
do not understand it. In eternity there is no before
and no after. Therefore, what happened a thousand
years ago and what will happen a thousand years from
now and what is now happening is one in eternity.
Therefore, what God did a thousand years ago and has

done and what he will do in a thousand years and what he
is now doing –– all this is nothing but one work.
Therefore a person who is risen beyond time into eternity
works with God what God worked a thousand years ago and
will work a thousand years hence.   This too is for wise
people a matter of knowledge and for ignorant people a
matter for belief.[34]

NOTES

1. Walter H. Capps, "Contemporary Socio-Political Change and the Work of Religious Studies," in Bulletin of the Council on the Study of Religion Waterloo, Wilfrid Laurier Univ. October 81 Vol. 12, no. 4 (October 1981).

2. Arnold Toynbee and Joyce Caplan, A Study of History, Oxford: Oxford University Press, 1972, p. 30.

3. Capps, "Contemporary Socio-Political Change."

4. Capps, "Contemporary Socio-Political Change."

5. R. Garaudy, Pour un Dialogue des civilisations, Paris: Denoel, 1977, p.7.

6. Garaudy, Pour un dialogue des civilisations, p. 7.

7. Garaudy, Pour un dialogue des civilisations, p. 7.

8. Richard L. Rubenstein, The Cunning of History, New York: Harper & Row, 1975, pp. 28-29.

9. Rubenstein, The Cunning of History, p. 29.

10. Theodore Roszak, Where the Wasteland Ends, New York: Anchor Books, 1973, pp. xv-xvi.

11. Roszak, Where the Wasteland Ends, p. xx.

12. Roszak, Where the Wasteland Ends, p. xx.

13. C. Jung, Psychological Reflections (edited by Jolande Jacobi), Princeton: Princeton University Press, 1978, pp. 14-15.

14. C. Jung, Psychology and The East, (translated by R.F.C. Hull), Princeton: Princeton University Press, 1978, p. 82.

15. Jung, Psychology and the East, p. 83.

16. Jung, Psychology and the East, pp. 84-85.

17. Jung, Psychology and the East, p. 81.

18. Hans Küng, "The World Religions in God's Plan of Salvation," in Christian Revelation and World Religions, Joseph Neuner, ed., London: Burns & Oates, 1967, p. 48.

19. Küng, "The World Religions in God's Plan of Salvation," p. 48.

20. Paul Archambault, L'Oeuvre Philosophique de Maurice Blondel, Paris: Bloud & Gay, 1928, p. 32.

21. Maurice Blondel, L'Action, Paris: Librairie Alcan, 1893, pp. 355-56.

22. Cicero, Scripta Quae Manserunt Omnia, part IV, vol. II: Laws 1, 10; also Oeuvres Complètes de Cicéron (translated by M. Nisard), Paris: Firmin-Didot et Cie, 1881; vol. IV, p. 369.

23. Paul Ricoeur, La Symbolique du Mal, Paris: Aubier, 1960, pp. 228-36.

24. Kala srjati bhutani kalah samharate prajah Samharantam prajah kalam kalah samayate punah.
Time creates (all) beings, Time destroys (all) creatures; (but) the Time which destroys (all) creatures is brought to an end (in its turn) by the (Great) Time.
Mahabharata, 1.1.248

25. Suttavibhanga, Parajika, I.1,4

26. Küng, "The World Religions in God's Plan," pp. 51-53.

27. G. Friedman, The Political Philosophy of the Frankfurt School, Ithaca, N.Y.: Cornell University Press, 1981, p. 112

28. Friedman, p. 112.

29. Friedman, p. 112.

30. Friedman, p. 112.

31. Carl Jung, <u>Modern Man in Search of A Soul</u>, New York: Harvest/H.B.J. Books, 1933, pp. 199-200.

32. Meister Eckhart, <u>Breakthrough</u>, Meister Eckhart's Creation Spirituality in New Translation, introduction and conclusion by Matthew Fox, New York: Doubleday, 1980, pp. 168, 465-66.

33. Fox, pp. 464-65.

34. Fox, p. 466.

CAN MODERNITY ACCOMMODATE TRANSCENDENCE?
Huston Smith

There are really two papers here -- one that answers no to the
question of whether modernity can accommodate transcendence, and a
second one that details the transcendence it excludes. But at the
outset, three disclaimers are necessary.

First, I will make no predictions. I haven't the foggiest idea
what's going to happen. On one side I find myself flanked by doomsday
Cassandras who see us in a moral meltdown; we are about to go down the
drain like Rome. On the other side the New Age Aquarians talk as if the
Gates of Eden will be opening for two-way traffic any day now. Frozen
on dead centre between them, I'd like to redirect, unopened, the mail I
receive from both sides to their opposite camps. Let them fight it out
while I hold their coats, for I have no idea what's in store.

Second, there will also be no historical comparisons: how our
present rates in comparison with other historical epochs. Is it better
to be living today than in the Middle Ages or Tang Dynasty China? What
I suspect is that of every epoch it could be said, as Dickens said of
the period in which he set his Tale of Two Cities, "It was the best of
times and the worst of times."

Third, I hope to steer clear of accusations, finger-pointing, and
blame. I would like not to add to the rhetoric of indictment. Recently
Germaine Greer lectured in Syracuse. Through the tone of her Female
Eunuch was strident, this time it was different. "There are no oppressors," she said; "there is oppression." There's something right about
that; if the leaders of the Russian Revolution had been more attuned to
it, history would be different. So if it appears as if I were nomina-
ting science or scientists for whipping-boys, that is not the case. It
is not "it" or "them" I am talking about; it is ourselves, all of us, an
historical phenomenon that we have stumbled into. Insofar as there is
responsibility, it devolves on us all. As Marianne Moore once said,
"There never was a war that was not inward."

With these propaedeutics out of the way, let me proceed now to the
substance of what I want to say, taking off from a point John Wilson
made in his paper:

> Note that we moved from remarking upon the modern as a
> given in contemporary life [that is, change has
> occurred] to identifying commitment to it as social

> modernization or cultural modernism; now with "moderni-
> ty," an additional move is made to reify this conscious-
> ness of social change so that it seems to have a content
> roughly equivalent to that similarly reified threat,
> "secularity."

Nicholls' response to this during the discussion that followed was that
he intended to reify continuously. I agreed, I don't think of secularity as epiphenomenon only. It is a phenomenon, a reality -- I wouldn't
even object to calling it an entity -- that feeds back causally on the
social institutions that helped generate it. Wilson thinks that "as
scholars ... we must resist this attribution of substantiality to attitudes and activities." I think I know what he means, but it is also
important to attribute substantiality to the sum of the attitudes and
activities we call secularity -- the kind of substantiality that pre-
pares us to see the causal input they have on history and the future.
The difference here may only reflect our disciplinary emphases, Wilson
the historian focusing on institutions and Nicholls and I on ideas; but
a substantive point is involved which the prejorative "reify" should not
be allowed to obscure.

For a definition of modernity, reified or not, I am content for
present purposes with one that appeared in The Chronicle of Higher
Education's review of Peter Berger's Facing up to Modernity: "If anything characterizes 'modernity,' it is a loss of faith in transcendence,
in a reality that encompasses but surpasses our quotidian affairs"
(Jan. 9, 1978). In a phrase Peter Berger himself introduced, modernity
is the non-sacred canopy that pervades the consciousness of contemporary
society.

From there we could proceed to a sociological analysis of what has
happened, pointing out that two important carriers of modernity have
been technological, industrial production on the one hand, and bureaucracy to facilitate that production on the other, but Berger has mapped
that route well, so there is no need to retrace it. Instead, I propose
to sketch the development that has occurred in the conceptual sphere.
What noetic, ideational carriers have contributed to the rise of
modernity?

Let me announce them by way of a diagram:

Logical Progression	Modernity's Version
anthropology	alienation
↑	↑
ontology (worldview)	naturalism
↑	↑
epistemology	empiricism
↑	↑
motivation	control

It is my thesis that, in the modern world at least, the logical progression has been in the direction the arrows indicate. We begin with motivations: what we want. On the basis of these wants we firm up -- crystallize -- ways of knowing that provide information for getting us to where we want to go. These epistemologies give rise in turn to ontologies, our notions of what is real; let X = knowledge, and with that the die is cast respecting worldview. Finally, anthropologies, in the broad sense of the way life feels, are conditioned by the worlds -- read "worldviews" -- into which life must fit.

With that formal model before us, I proceed now to fill in the specifics for the passing of the Western world into the period that has come to be called modernity. If we read the story backwards, beginning with consequences and probing beneath them to the causes that brought them into being, we reverse the direction of the arrows. The distinctive feel of modern life, alienation, arises in important part from its dominant worldview, naturalism. This in turn is the product of modernity's controlling epistemology, empiricism, which has moved stage centre because, as the epistemology that best serves science, it augments the control modernity is committed to.

Generative Sequence	Modernity's Version
anthropology	alienation
↑	↓
ontology (world view)	naturalism
↑	↓
epistemology	empiricism
↑	↓
motivation	control

I do not, of course, see this as a private, idiosyncratic reading of the situation, but as an objective report of what has happened. To argue that point I shall introduce a supporting "brief" for each of the four steps of the consequence I have outlined.

1. Beginning with anthropology or the way life feels, a respected sociologist, Manfred Stanley, reports that "it is by now a Sunday-supplement commonplace that the ... modernization of the world is accompanied by a spiritual malaise that has come to be called alienation."[1]

2. For the cause of this alienation, Stanley turns to the modern worldview, or _ontology_:

> At its most fundamental level, the diagnosis of aliena-
> tion is based on the view that modernization forces upon
> us a world that, although baptized as real by science,
> is denuded of all humanly recognizable qualities; beauty
> and ugliness, love and hate, passion and fulfilment,
> salvation and damnation. It is not, of course, being
> claimed that such matters are not part of the existen-
> tial realities of human life. It is rather that the
> scientific world view makes it illegitimate to speak of
> them as being "objectively" part of the world, forcing
> us instead to define such evaluation and such emotional
> experience as "merely subjective" projections of
> people's inner lives.

> The world, once an "enchanted garden" to use Max Weber's
> memorable phrase, has now become disenchanted, deprived
> of purpose and direction, bereft -- in these senses --
> of life itself. All that which is allegedly basic to
> the specifically human status in nature, comes to be
> forced back upon the precincts of the "subjective"
> which, in turn, is pushed by the modern scientific view
> ever more into the province of dreams and illusions.[2]

3. Ernest Gellner pinpoints the _epistemology_ that produced the naturalistic worldview just described. For something to be believed in today's West, it must pass two tests. First, "there is the empiricist insistence that [it] stand ready to be judged by ... something reason- ably close to the ordinary notion of 'experience'. Second, there is the 'mechanistic' insistence on impersonal ... explanations."[3]

4. Why do we assume that only beliefs that are supported by mechanism and empiricism are true? Gellner is frank in grounding the reason in our _motivation_. Truth of the kind that is supported by mechanism and empiricism augments our power to control.

> We have of course no guarantee that the world must be
> such as to be amenable to such explanations; we can only
> show that we are constrained to think so. It was Kant's

merit to see that this compulsion is in us, not in
things. It was Weber's to see that it is historically a
specific kind of mind, not human mind as such, which is
subject to this compulsion. What it amounts to is in
the end simple: if there is to be effective knowledge or
explanation at all, it must have this form, for any
other kind of "explanation" ... is ipso facto powerless.

We have become habituated to and dependent on
effective knowledge, and hence have bound ourselves to
this kind of genuine explanation.... "Reductionism," the
view that everything in the world is really something
else, and that something else is coldly impersonal, is
simply the ineluctable corollary of effective explanation. [4]

Gellner closes the circle of the logic I am exposing by admitting,
with Manfred Stanley, the anthropological hazards of this epistemic
move:

It was also Kant's merit to see the inescapable price of
this Faustian purchase of real (sic) knowledge. [In
delivering] cognitive effectiveness [it] exacts its
inherent moral, "dehumanizing" price.... The price of
real knowledge is that our identities, freedom, norms,
are no longer underwritten by our vision and comprehen-
sion of things. [5]

In the same vein, Hannah Arendt links the anthropology of modernity to
its worldview with a perceptiveness that warrants quoting her at some
length.

What has come to an end is the distinction between the
sensual and the supersensual, together with the notion,
at least as old as Parmenides, that whatever is not
given to the senses...is more real, more truthful, more
meaningful than what appears; that it is not just beyond
sense perception but above the world of the senses.
Meanwhile, in increasingly strident voices, the few
defenders of metaphysics have warned us of the danger of
nihilism inherent in this development; and although they

themselves seldom invoke it, they have an important
argument in their favor: it is indeed true that once the
suprasensual realm is discarded, its opposite, the world
of appearances as understood for so many centuries, is
also annihilated. The sensual, as still understood by
the positivists, cannot survive the death of the supersensual. No one knew this better than Nietzsche who,
with his poetic and metaphoric description of the assas-
sination of God in Zarathustra, has caused so much
confusion in these matters. In a significant passage in
The Twilight of Idols, he clarifies what the word God
meant in Zarathustra. It was merely a symbol for the
suprasensual realm as understood by metaphysics; he now
uses instead of God the word true world and says: "We
have abolished the true world. What has remained? The
apparent one perhaps? On no! With the true world we
have also abolished the apparent one."[6]

Though I have yet to say so explicitly, I think it is clear that it
was modern science that inaugurated the development I have been describing. In the sixteenth and seventeenth centuries the West stumbled on a
way of knowing -- roughly the scientific method -- which quickly produced remarkable results. Quite apart from its noetic yield, it found
ways to multiply goods, relieve drudgery, and (a little later) improve
health and extend life-expectancy. As these are not inconsiderable
gains, it's no wonder that the West went for them and for the control
that made them posssible. "Here I sell what everyone wants: power,"
Matthew Bolton, James Watt's partner, posted in his machine shop. That
the power was over nature, not over one's self, seemed at the time like
a detail. The West lined up to buy what Watt and Bolton offered.

This is the point where, as I said in my preamble, I would like to
avoid a polemical tone. I do not wish to be understood as attacking the
scientific method and condemning its truth, beauty, and fruitfulness off
which I live so very well. It's just that the epistemology that produces those fruits cannot cover the waterfront. There are regions of
life that refuse to appear in its viewfinder. Dropping metaphor, let me
note four things that science -- I am speaking of science in its modern,
English-speaking sense -- cannot deal with.

1. Intrinsic and normative values. Science can deal with instru-
mental values (smoking is injurious to your health), but whether the

intrinsic value, health, is preferable to immediate somatic gratification, it cannot say. Likewise, it can work with descriptive values --
what people do like; opinion polls and market research are exact sciences. But what they should like (normative values) it cannot adjudicate.

2. Purposes. Jacques Monod says point-blank that "the cornerstone
of scientific method is...the systematic denial that 'true' knowledge
can be got at by interpreting phenomena in terms of final causes -- that
is to say, of 'purpose'."[7] Francis Bacon saw that this exclusion was
imperative if science were to get on with its job. He likened final
causes to virgins -- beautiful but barren. They produce nothing in the
way of knowledge that furthers control.

3. Meanings. Science is meaningful throughout, but there are two
kinds of meanings it cannot deal with: global meanings (what is the
meaning of life?), and existential meanings, the kind that comes to view
when we ask if something is meaningful. Meaningful truths involve us,
but there's no way that science can guarantee that its discoveries will
draw us in. However stupendous its announcements, we are always at
liberty to shrug our shoulders, turn on our heels, and walk away. If we
are depressed, we are likely to do just that.

4. Qualities. Science can deal with the measurable substrates that
underlie certain qualities -- the lightwaves that are correlated with
the sensation blue, for example -- but the experience of blueness itself
it cannot penetrate.

I find that people don't like to admit the existence of extra-
scientific domains, yet their existence is so obvious when you stop to
think about them that the fact that they are not common knowledge
suggests that we have chosen not to think about them. It would be
frightening to think that the epistemic probe on which modernity has
staked its existence is fallible. So even when these limitations of the
scientific method are pointed out, they are excused as being temporary.
Don't we have to learn to stand before we can walk, and to walk before
we can run? Science is still in its infancy; in time it will master
these four subjects in the way it has now mastered nature. This excuse
needs to be met head-on, beginning with the observation that it is
becoming more strained with each passing decade. True, modern science
hasn't been around as long as art or religion, but it wasn't born
yesterday. The fact that for more than three hundred years, while
humanity has all but held its breath, science hasn't advanced a milli-
meter into these four domains should prepare us to face what I personally now consider an objective fact: science is not an instrument that can

deal with those kinds of things. The next time you encounter this plea for more time, I hope you will ask how much longer we need wait before asking if this particular egg is going to hatch.

Everything I have said thus far relates to the first half of my project, the pointing out of why the modern ethos can't accommodate transcendence. It can't do so because it was crafted by a device, the scientific method, whose power stands in exact proportion to its limitations. Its power enlists our commitment; its limitations we hide from ourselves because they threaten that commitment. I detailed science's limitations by noting four kinds of things it cannot work with, but I can compress these into a single restriction that relates directly to my title. Science can work only with things that are inferior to us. For the crux of science is the controlled experiment, and we can only control our subordinates. The controlled experiment can, of course, work with things that exceed us in certain respects -- in size, say, or brute physical power. But I am talking about things that are greater than we are in every respect, including intelligence, freedom, and whatever other attributes you might wish to enter. What might higher beings who exceed us in every respect be? Extra-terrestrial intelligences more advanced than ourselves? Angels? God? What is clear is that if there are such beings, there is no way that they will fit into our controlled experiments. If they exist, they dance circles around us, not we them.

So nothing greater than ourselves can make its way into a scientific worldview, which is simply another way of saying that modernity cannot accommodate transcendence.

What, other than that it is greater than ourselves, can be said about this transcendence modernity excludes? I have tried to answer that question in my Forgotten Truth. Here there is room for only the briefest summary.

With negligible exceptions, every outlook anthropologists and historians have discovered has distinguished this world from Another World: appearance from Reality, the Absolute from the relative, phenomena from Noumena. India refers to this world as maya, Australian aborigines call the Absolute the Dreaming, but there is no need to enter a long list. What is important is that both of these realms need in turn to be subdivided.

This world divides into the visible and the invisible. The second of these, the invisible, begins with sensations, thoughts, and feelings that are undeniable though they don't connect with our physical senses. Today in the West these invisibles end with our internal states, for science can't really deal with them and they are countenanced only because direct experience won't let us rule them out; at least they exist subjectively. Traditionally, though, the invisible aspects of ourselves were simply points where the invisible world at large washed through us. Through ghosts and spirits, whether evil or good, the objective invisible was, for traditional man, a conspicuous part of the world in which we daily live. Whether modernity is right in withdrawing the sentience of the traditional world into the bodies of animate creatures, leaving thereby the rest of nature a "bare, ruin'd choir" of dead matter and primary qualities, is one of the unanswered questions of our time.

As for the Other World, the division it calls for is less obvious but no less real. Aspects of the World can be known, but in the end it bottoms out into mystery, one that can be neither conceived nor precisely articulated. Here we encounter East Asia's Tao that can and cannot be spoken, the Brahma that has (saguna) and has not (nirguna) attributes, and the Godhead of apophatic and negative theology which, in its radical ineffability, must be distinguished from, or rather added to, the God of Abraham, Isaac, and Jacob.

This four-fold structure of reality is so pervasive that I ventured in Forgotten Truth to call it primordial tradition. By my lights it is not only generic but true, but I have not tried to argue that case here. The higher links of this great chain of being, the ones that comprise the Other World, are what I mean by transcendence. Modernity cannot accommodate transcendence in this sense that is what I have here tried to show here.

NOTES

1. Manfred Stanley, "Beyond progress: Three post-political futures," in
    Robert Bundy (ed.), Images of the Future: the Twenty-first Century
    and Beyond, Buffalo, N.Y.: Prometheus, 1976, p. 115.

2. Stanley, "Beyond Progress," p.115.

3. Ernest Gellner, The Legitimation of Belief, London and New York:
    Cambridge University Press, 1974, p. 206.

4. Gellner, The Legitimation of Belief, pp. 206-207.

5. Gellner, The Legitimation of Belief, p. 207.

6. Hannah Arendt, "Thinking and Moral Consideration," Social Research
    38 (Autumn 1971): p. 420.

7. Jacques Monod, Chance and Necessity; an essay on the natural philo-
    sophy of modern biology, translated by Austryn Wainhouse, New York:
    Vintage, 1972, p. 21.

IMMANENT TRANSCENDENCE: SPIRITUALITY IN A SCIENTIFIC AND CRITICAL AGE

William Nicholls

The modern world is the world of TV pictures from Saturn, of jet travel, two cars in almost every household, of calculators and computers and stereo sets, of central heating, of heart transplants and exponential population increase. It is the world where the top celebrities are entertainers, where the best-selling videocassettes are pornographic, where children of both sexes are prostituted in our cities, while psychologists defend incest as beneficial for children, in which two-thirds of the world's population is so poor that they can barely survive at all, while many of the remaining third are richer by far than the kings and nobles of former times. It is also the world of Auschwitz and of Hiroshima.

What do these and other equally familiar aspects of the world we live in have in common? Is there some factor or set of factors of which they are all equally the product? We can safely reply that there is. The world we know is the product of the liberated intelligence of human beings -- liberated, that is, from both the limitations and the restraints imposed by religious mythology and sacred law. It is also in very large measure the product of the logical-analytical intellect disconnected from feeling and intuition, including ethical and spiritual intuition. It is the work of intelligence in the service of the ego. At its best, this kind of intelligence can produce marvellous artifacts which can enrich human life. It can also degenerate into cunning, devising efficacious means for the enactment of lust, hatred, and cruelty.

This is the world over which Nietzsche's saying "God is dead" holds good everywhere. The death of God preceded Auschwitz and Hiroshima by perhaps a century, but the former was the necessary condition for the latter, and for what may still follow. Since that time, "everything is permitted." And what can and may be done, sooner or later will be done. Hell has made its appearance on the surface of the earth, and man has done little to repel it. Those who cling to the remnants of traditional religion, even if they (dishonestly) designate themselves a moral majority, are as powerless as the rest of us to change the conditions under which they and we live. Candidates for the presidency of the United States now find it necessary to profess that they have been born again, but this rebirth will not, it seems, stay their hand from the red button.

In face of such realities, a person of any sensitivity may be appalled and wish for a return to a society in which God was believed to rule, and his law enforced by all the institutions of society, even though this return were to be accomplished at the sacrifice of the enormous freedoms and benefits that modernity has brought to us, if not to the rest of the world. We have seen what happens when that is attempted, in Khomeini's Iran. There is no good reason to believe that man in a theocratic society was or would now be less barbarous than modern man. The only difference is that in such a society barbarity is carried out in the name of the one true God, beside whom there is no other. Perhaps there, however, we may hope that there will be some restraint, unknown where his name is not uttered, which may hold back another Auschwitz. But if I were an Iranian Jew (or a Baha'i), I would not bank on it.

It is one thing to wish for a return from modernity to a traditional society. It is another thing to accomplish it. Unless modernity collapses as a result of economic ruin or thermonuclear holocaust, it does not seem likely that we will be able to return to a traditional society whose myths and laws derive from a great religion of revelation. Those who judge that living in a traditional, religiously determined society would on balance be to the greater benefit of humanity cannot recreate, by means of their own thoughts and activities as a minority within a modernized society, a civilization that took a whole society many centuries and perhaps even millennia to build up, and has not existed in Western Europe or North America for two and a half centuries at least. In fact, since there is no such thing as traditional religion in the modernized societies in which we all live, none of us has ever experienced what it is like to live under it. Even in Japan, it appears that modernization has proceeded so far and so fast that it is doubtful if more than remnants of traditional religion persists.

On the contrary, all so-called orthodoxies, including Jewish and Christian ones, are really neo-orthodoxies, reactive phenomena engendered by the modern world itself, and bearing its marks in their unavoidable awareness of pluralism, and their basis, not in social forces, but in the autonomous choices of individuals to belong to them. Living by a consciously adopted neo-orthodoxy may permit one to pretend, at any rate for religious purposes, that modernity is not there and has never happened. But that does not stop one being a modern person and experiencing even religion in a modern way. Since modernity cannot be excluded from daily life, even if perhaps it can be to some extent from the practice of religion, such a person experiences a dichotomy between religion and the rest of life which was unknown in traditional societies. This dichotomy is itself characteristically modern, and cannot be avoided while modernity prevails. It appears to me that the effects of modernity upon religion are therefore irreversible, except by a catastrophe destroying the structures upon which a modernized culture rests. It need hardly be said that we ought not to wish for such a catastrophe in the name of religion, though many people today, including myself, believe that its advent is by no means unlikely if some basic spiritual changes do not occur in the modernized world. Part of our question is whether such changes can realistically be looked for, or worked for.

I conclude that modernity is the reality within which we ourselves must live our present embodied existence in space and time. I do not of course mean by that that modernity should be regarded as real in an ultimate sense. In that sense, no society is more real than any other. All societies are relatively real, and no more. Ours has no more ultimate validity than others, but that insight does not remove us from it. In any case, we cannot escape from this relative reality by fantasizing about a past golden age or a future earthly paradise, the temptations of spiritually minded people in the one case and of revolutionary utopians in the other. We must live where we are, or not at all. Perhaps by withdrawing our energies from fantasies about past or future societies, we can do something to improve this one. Even if our own here-and-now were much more favourable to the spiritual dimension of man than appears to be the case, it would still be necessary to transcend it through non-attachment even to these spiritual benefits.

If this reasoning is valid, there is little to be gained by celebrating the modern world, on the one hand, as liberation from the shackles of dead religion, or bemoaning it, on the other, as a kali yuga, in contrast to more religiously oriented periods in history, as if these periods did not also occur within the same kali yuga. Either, or more probably both, of these judgments may be well founded. But making them may not be of much help in answering what appear to me to be even more urgent questions: Is there a spiritual dimension in man which is not bound to any particular culture, and therefore can be discovered even in a non-religious one such as our own? In other words, is it possible to realize this spiritual dimension under the conditions of modernity, within which we have to live? If we conclude that it is possible, how is it to be done? And finally, what can be done in the absence of traditional religion to raise the ethical and spiritual level of society as a whole? These are the questions with which I struggle, and the present paper is yet another attempt to give myself and any other interested persons some fragments of answers to them.

The question of whether man is inherently spiritual seems to be avoided, to a considerable extent, in the discipline of religious studies, under the (at present very powerful) influence of anthropologically oriented methodologies. Religion is seen as a socially constituted imaginative and intellectual structure, providing reality and meaning for a society through its myths and rituals. It follows that each religion is relative both to the society by which it is constituted and also, in another sense, to all other religions. But its relation to ultimate reality, or even to any possible essence of man which transcends culture, cannot be considered within the limits of such methodologies, or perhaps within the present intellectual contract which unites academic people. In the university, we all experience a powerful taboo against asking, and still more against daring to answer, ultimate questions of this sort. Not even philosophers will attempt it any more. For us as students of religion, the issue is even more confused by the fear, which we ourselves share, of proselytism for a particular religion under the guise of academic study. If we avoid these questions, however, we are really demolishing the raison d'etre of our own discipline. Anthropology can do the job, and what it cannot do, the history of ideas or sociology can well enough undertake. But it is not a matter of opinion whether a spiritual dimension is intrinsic to human nature, and answering it in the affirmative would not make us anti-intellectual fundamentalists, though it would be very threatening to many or most of our colleagues. No other discipline will ask, still less answer, this question if we do not. If the answer is negative, and the currently popular methodologies really assume a negative answer, if only by what they do not take into account, I question whether our discipline has a justification for an independent existence, in the university or anywhere else.

It is not just methodologies that maintain a significant silence about anything in man which transcends cultural conditioning. As modernity has developed in the whole intellectual subculture which dominates the university at present, it has become a matter of unquestioned and therefore tacit agreement that man does not possess an essence which is situated beyond the influence of cultural forces. Man is considered as a mind, and this mind is a social product. Even

feelings are regarded as learned responses to social conditioning. We
do not have to be Marxists to take this social and relativistic view.
Unconsciously, the far right takes it too, when it implicitly refuses to
acknowledge a common humanity with those who live in the Soviet Union
and subscribe to its ideology. Not only for Communists but for Reagan-
ites, socialist man is a different kind of human being. The relativism
and pluralism which we all identify as characteristics of modernity
imply that man is the product of the culture within which he lives. If
so, it would be meaningless to look for an essence of man, and spirituality, as I am already implicitly defining it, would become impossible.
Religion could be discussed from this perspective, but spirituality
could not, except as an aspect of religious thought and behaviour. Yet
I have said that modernity is inescapable. How can this dilemma be
overcome?

Let me start boldly. Asking the question of a spiritual essence in
man actually answers it.[1] We could not ask the question of whether
there is anything in us which is beyond our conditioning except from a
standpoint of what is not conditioned. If we did not transcend our
conditioning, we should be unable to do otherwise than affirm the
reality and truth of what we are conditioned to regard as real and
true. The critical capacity in us, which permits us to doubt the
validity of our own convictions, belongs to a level in us that already
transcends that extremely large area which is susceptible to conditioning. The very search that causes us to ask the classic, existential
questions Who am I? and What is real? is evidence of a level of consciousness, an identity, which is more real than the products of social
conditioning. The fact that we search for spirituality, even if we do
not seem to be attaining it, is evidence that we are spiritual. The
beginning of our spirituality lies in making contact with that spiritual
essence within us that searches beyond what our own culture presents us
with, looking for what abides unchanged through all cultural diversity
and development. Once we have recognized it in ourselves, we cannot
fail to recognize it in others, across all cultural barriers. These
affirmations are clearly not the outcome of empiricist reasoning. They
are existential or intuitive. But if we are not willing to affirm them,
we are conniving at the diminution and ultimately the destruction of our
humanity.

In affirming that we ourselves, and all human beings, possess -- or
better, are actually constituted as human by -- a spiritual essence, we
are suggesting that the modern world does not preclude and may even

encourage the adoption of a transcendental position, in spite of the fact that it notoriously makes it very difficult to envisage the possibility of transcendence. The collapse of the transcendence of Being (Heidegger), or the death of God (Nietzsche), is an almost inescapable feature of the consciousness we share as members of a modernized culture. The absence, or "eclipse,"[2] of exterior transcendence does not seem, however, to rule out a <u>transcendental</u> consciousness, that is, a standpoint or locus of awareness which permits us to break our customary identification with the conditioned mind we normally regard as our identity, and in this way to see what previously had appeared to be subjective as objective. We can, it appears, transcend our conditioned cultural identity, even if that identity is modern. At the moment that we decide to observe it and analyse the way in which it has come into being, we have ceased to identify with it, at least for that particular moment. For the duration of that act of self-observation, we have identified with a transcendental consciousness within ourselves.

Is there some logical contradiction here? Does the affirmation of one sense of transcendence in fact entail the affirmation of the other, which we have just conceded is apparently precluded by modernity? Or does the denial of the one involve the denial of the other? Perhaps. If so, the affirmation of what I have chosen to call provisionally "immanent transcendence" may prove to be for us moderns the way back to transcendence in the traditional sense. However, such a conclusion would certainly be premature at this point. I am not going to argue metaphysically, but existentially, as I understand it. I want to consider what our experience actually is as modern people, and I am trying to speak about existence as I and others experience it.

A characteristic of modernity that has been very frequently singled out for attention, especially by European writers, is autonomy.[3] We have already begun to touch on this topic, at the beginning of the paper where I spoke of the modern world as the product of the liberated intelligence of human beings, liberated from both the restraints and the limitations of a sacred order. At that point I was concerned to emphasize the ambiguity of this liberation, the extraordinary extent of its consequences for evil as well as for good. In returning to the topic now, I want to emphasize a more traditional point, the contrast between heteronomy and autonomy. Autonomy has both an intellectual and an ethical aspect. Intellectually, it leads to the scientific spirit of enquiry, embodying the principle of learning from experience of reality instead of relying on mythology or dogma. In this sense, autonomy means free thinking, in all the connotations of the phrase. Ethically, as Kant showed once and for all, it means free adherence to moral law because that law is perceived as inherently right and categorically binding. It would be just as binding even if there were no divine lawgiver -- _etsi deus non daretur_, in the phrase from Grotius which so struck Dietrich Bonhoeffer.

A dramatic example of such autonomy is to be found in a famous baritone aria from Verdi's _La forza del destino_, composed in 1862, "Morir! Tremenda cosa: Urna fatale del mio destino." The singer is Don Carlo di Vargas, who is engaged in a vendetta to remove the dishonour to his blood, or family name, caused by the death of his father, and (as Carlo supposes) the seduction of his sister Leonora, at the hands of the half-Inca, Don Alvaro. In the course of the complicated and not altogether convincing plot of the opera, Don Alvaro and Don Carlo, each in disguise and under an assumed name, meet and become sworn friends, as a result of Alvaro saving the life of Carlo. Soon afterwards Alvaro is himself wounded in battle and apparently at the point of death. He entrusts to Carlo a sealed package of papers which, he says, contain a secret that must die with him. Carlo is to burn the package unopened as soon as Alvaro is dead. This he has solemnly sworn to do in the name of friendship. Now, however, Carlo has begun to suspect the true identity of his friend. During the recitative, "Morir! Tremenda cosa," we find Carlo pondering his paradoxical situation, with the key to the knowledge of the dying man's identity placed by destiny in his hand, but restrained by the trust placed in him by his friend from taking advantage of the situation. He thinks of breaking the seal and looking at the papers. Perhaps the action would be justifiable if the dying man did turn out to be the killer of his father and the seducer of his sister, the "cursed Indian" who has defiled his blood. He reaches to open the package: there is no one to see him. Suddenly he experiences an ethical revulsion, vividly and dramatically portrayed in the music, and he cries: "No? Ben mi vegg' io." (No one to see me? _I_ see me!) He throws down the envelope, unable to open it. Soon, however, the obsessive passion of the vendetta gets the better of him after all, and he is able to discover an ethically acceptable way of finding out Alvaro's real identity and linking him with Leonora. With this we are not now concerned.

Perhaps I see more in that "Ben mi vegg' io" than Verdi or his librettist Piave consciously intended, dramatic as the moment is when entrusted to a good singer. I cannot help reading into it something

that has, no doubt, no real place in the rather mediaeval story of
honour and dishonour, of blood feud and family vendetta. Carlo's flash
of insight that he is responsible to himself, more than to the external
authority of a social obligation to avenge his sister's chastity, is
authentically modern and post-Kantian. But in the actual language in
which it is expressed, as well as in Verdi's powerful musical response
to the moment, I find something deeper still, which will serve to introduce the point I now want to make. Carlo has experienced the paradox of
self-observation. If only for an instant, he has become the observer of
his own thoughts and actions, and judges them in the light of an ethical
principle which he has fully internalized and made his own. He is
experiencing ethical self-transcendence, and thus connecting with a much
deeper level of his own selfhood than, perhaps, he has experienced
before. He is on the verge of actualizing what the Indian psychologies
call _viveka_, the power of discrimination between the real and the
unreal. _Viveka_ in turn is a function of that in us which is called the
observer, the first manifestation in consciousness of the true Self. It
is to be noted that whereas this I can see the other I, the normal
subject of thoughts and behaviour, thereby objectifying an identity
which was formerly subjective, the observing I (or eye) cannot be
objectified; it can only be known by identification. This identity is
already non-dual.

Autonomy, or responsibility for oneself and one's actions, is
evidently not yet the same as _viveka_, or discrimination between the real
and the unreal, any more than the moral conscience is necessarily identical with the transcending Self. But they are not far apart, and the
one is a natural avenue to the other. Autonomy can lead to spiritual
self-transcendence. Such responsibility for oneself is widely recognized by people today, and often appealed to by those who hope to enlist
others in bringing about desirable changes in society, as well as, for
another example, in psychotherapy. If I am responsible for my own
ethical standards, or more precisely for my own free acceptance of
universal ethical laws, I am likewise responsible for my actions and for
the situations which they create. I cannot plead to myself, at any
rate, that someone else prevented me from taking constructive actions,
whether by external prohibitions or by earlier commands that have by now
been internalized in the psyche. Nor, as the Nazi war-criminals found
at Nuremberg, can I any longer excuse my actions when obeying orders.
My responsibility to the State, it was then agreed, though the lesson
has apparently been widely forgotten, does not override my responsi-

bility to myself. Plenty of people, including many in positions of
power, fail to rise to this level of personal responsibility, but we are
aware of its existence, and we know that in the end we cannot escape
it. The modern development of culture has liberated us from heterono-
mous sacred law, but in doing so has placed full responsibility in our
own hands.

We are likewise responsible today for our own spiritual life. Here
the profounder sense of self-awareness, just discussed, comes more fully
into play. Such glimpses as I have attributed to Don Carlo di Vargas in
the opera, La forza del destino, may convince us that we have the
capacity to rise above our conditioning, cultural or individual, and the
manifold temptations of the mind, to make a connection with something
more real and permanent in ourselves. In order to do this, we do not
need, though we may be assisted by, an external framework of symbolism
and sacred law. We already possess within ourselves a capacity for
distinguishing between the real and the unreal, and therefore for discerning the spiritual path, even when, as nowadays, it is very difficult
to make out.

As I tell my first-year students in religious studies, Ernest
Hemingway, asked on one occasion what writers need most, is said to have
replied: "A bullshit indicator." They need to know when they are
writing bullshit and when they are writing truthfully and authentically. Writers do know this, and that is why they so often go through many
drafts of their work before they, or their indicator, are satisfied. We
all have such an indicator, and we need it not just for art but for
life. We need at all times to know when we are being phony and when we
are being real. The indicator never fails to emit its signal, red or
green, but we do not always allow ourselves to look. An important
aspect of a contemporary spiritual path is training ourselves to be
aware of, and open at all times to, the signals of this built-in
"bullshit indicator."

In this sense, it is not possible to enter a spiritual path because
someone else, even God, tells us to. Nor does it make any sense to do
it in the hope of some future reward, or of avoiding punishment. You
have to choose spirituality because you actually prefer it, because you
find it expresses your own nature. Loyalty to ourselves is our highest
and, perhaps in the last resort, only loyalty. There is a parallel to
this modern experience in the rather frequently encountered sayings of
the esoteric spiritual writers of the past, who insist that God is never
to be sought out of fear of hell or hope of heaven. If he is not loved

for himself, he is not loved at all. The modern experience of autonomy
and personal responsibility opens on to a spiritual way that has in the
past been regarded as esoteric, in contrast to an exoteric religiousness
where personal salvation was the central issue. The autonomous modern
person is not concerned with future salvation. Such a person is concerned with truth and authenticity in the present, and with the responsible actions to which these lead. We may even say, along with
Bonhoeffer, that such a person is not concerned with salvation at all in
any traditional, religious sense. Granted, many people do not appear to
be concerned with spirituality either, but if they are, it is to be
expected that it will be in this autonomous sense.

It may be justifiably argued that the modern recognition of the
relativity of cultures, referred to earlier, is a purely intellectual
act, which in no way implies the opening up of the transcendental awareness we have been discussing. The same can be true of ethical autonomy,
which can be discussed in purely rational and intellectual terms, as it
often is by philosophers, who want everything to be rational. On the
other hand, only if there actually is such a transcendental awareness
can we speak of a spiritual essence in man which transcends all cultures
and therefore is attainable even under the conditions of modernity. The
usual implication of cultural relativity is precisely that man lacks an
essence transcending culture. Likewise autonomy can be used as an
argument for moral relativity, though I have not used it in that way
here. These objections are valid up to a point. Certainly it cannot be
claimed that an intellectual recognition of the relativity of one's own
culture, or even of one's personal ego identity, is the same as transcending one's mind and seeing the identity we have clung to, modern or
otherwise, as a conditioned artifact. Transcending the ego is an existential act, not an intellectual theory.

Nevertheless, this difficulty is not peculiar to modernity. Even a
traditional religious culture could not confer spirituality upon anyone
simply by the fact of participation in it. No culture can do that for
anyone. The question raised here is whether the formative ideas of a
culture can provide some kind of opening towards the spiritual dimension. It is generally believed that the symbolic systems of traditional
societies, their mythological portrayal of a multi-storied universe,
representing the hierarchy of being, provided an opening for the recognition of exterior transcendence. The modern world appears to have
closed that way for us. But if a culture cannot of itself bring about a
spiritual realization, it must follow that some other culture cannot

preclude it. In closing one door, the modern world may actually have opened another, at least by a chink. I am suggesting that just as the mythological picture of a multi-storied universe may have served in the past to open the door for a recognition of external transcendence, the modern recognition of cultural relativity may serve to open the door for a transcendental awareness of one's own relativity. We have agreed that the opening of a door does not of itself propel anyone through the opening. But our own experience and that of others surely confirms this connection between the recognition that we are conditioned by our culture, in itself an intellectual process, and the further existential act of choosing to identify instead with the transcendental awareness of our identity as conditioned. This choice, which is not made once and for all, but from moment to moment, is spiritual.

To see not only our culture and our morality but everything we are accustomed to regard as our identity as the conditioned product of external forces that have temporarily shaped us is no small step. Indeed, it is rather like death, and probably if it is our destiny to be fully conscious at the time of our own death it will seem like the dissolution of that same conditioned artifact. What will then be left? Nothing objective, but that awareness, which is present even now when we temporarily transcend our conditioned mind. This awareness belongs, I believe, to the spiritual essence within human beings, which is not the product of culture, and therefore cannot be taken away from us by any cultural changes. As soon as we join it, we are released from the bonds of modernity, and we know that it cannot be a spiritual prison, any more than any other culture. If then, on the basis of this experience of self-transcendence, we choose to affirm the reality of the spiritual essence of man, we can be confident that we are not taking up inauthentically the standpoint of a culture that is past and gone, or of some hoped-for future age that has not yet dawned. We are rather bearing witness to the experiential reality of something that is already conceded intellectually by many of our contemporaries, even if they have not made the same experiment in consciousness. It might even be possible to claim that modernity favours this insight or awareness to a somewhat greater degree than the dogmatic, esoteric religious cultures of the past, which were characterized by an uncompromising emphasis upon an externally transcedent God who was in many ways constructed in the image of an earthly parent. Such a God is really an idol, which has to disappear from consciousness along the spiritual path, to be replaced by the darkness of "unknowing" -- in many ways so like the darkness we moderns inhabit -- the darkness in which alone the true reality which men have named as God can be obscurely sensed.

In making this connection between the dark night of Christian mysticism and the darkness of the modern consciousness, I am borrowing from the ideas of someone who profoundly influenced me when I was a student at Cambridge thirty-five years ago. The open lectures of H.A. Hodges, Professor of Philosophy at the University of Reading, made a deep and lasting impression on me and many others, and in retrospect I can see that Hodges influenced me and continues to influence me far more than any of my regular teachers. He suggested to us that the whole critical movement in philosophy, which demolished the metaphysical structures which had corresponded to the traditional mythological picture of the universe, could be seen as introducing modern man to what he called a "dark night of the intellect." As in the case of the dark nights described by St. John of the Cross, Hodges' "night of the intellect" is purgative, or purifying. That is to say, it purifies those who can accept it without giving up their trust in the ultimately spiritual character of reality from idolatrous attachments to concepts, releasing them for union with the Reality which is beyond all idols. What is beyond idols, said Hodges, echoing Pascal, is not the God of the philosophers, but the God of Abraham, Isaac, and Jacob, the inalienably invisible one who is known only by trust. (A very brief sketch of these and many other seminal ideas is contained in Hodges' little book, which covers the same ground as the Cambridge lectures, entitled Christianity and the Modern World View.) [4]

When the night descends upon spiritual searchers, it is tempting for them to despair and conclude that behind the darkness there is not merely not the God of one's former exoteric beliefs and devotional experience, but simply nothing at all. This is of course the road that the majority of moderns have taken. But it is not the only possible one. St. John of the Cross tells us that genuine contemplatives -- today we might call such people motivated searchers -- do not give up the search or turn for satisfaction to sensual comforts, but patiently wait in the darkness of faith, clinging with the will to the God they cannot know with the intellect. Thay are no longer able to think discursively about God, at least while meditating, but they can adhere to him by mantra-like acts of faith, love, and surrender to his will. In this spiritual desert there is no satisfaction for the senses, i.e., for religious devotion, nor for the intellect, but the will of the contemplative is able to find peace there.

Hodges suggests a second way of viewing our spiritual experience in the modern world, therefore, and I want to relate it to the one I have already begun to discuss. We might say that my earlier emphasis on transcending as opposed to transcendence owes something to Asian ways of spirituality, while Hodges' talk about the night of the intellect belongs to the Western, and specifically the Catholic, tradition of spirituality. But ultimately there is only one humanity and one spirituality. If Hodges was right, the collapse of the transcendence of Being, or the "death of God," can be considered, existentially rather than metaphysically, as the night of the intellect. This night is perhaps as dark as those through which Catholic contemplatives had to learn to walk under the guidance of such teachers as St. John of the Cross. But according to these teachers, this darkness is much closer to the truth than the bright religious light which had preceded it. For those who continue to trust, it is an initiation into a new way of knowing the Divine, by union instead of by means of the conventional subject-object structure. The theme of darkness, of unknowing, in Christian spirituality goes back at least to Pseudo-Denys, and behind him to the neo-Platonists, if not to earlier Christian tradition stemming from the desert hermits. The neo-Platonists were quite clear that the One could not be known by ordinary consciousness, operating within the subject-object structure. The One could be known only in ecstasy, by a union in which the subject and the object both disappear for the instant of ecstasy and all that is present is One. Such a moment of union cannot be thought while it is happening, and any description of it outside the ecstatic moment is and can be only theoretical.[5] However, if the One is in this sense a non-dual reality, any attempt to know It as an object must fail. If God disappears from man's consciousness as an object of thought or religious devotion, that disappearance is not an error of thought or a religious failure; it is the result of a closer approach to the truth, a truth that no spiritual seeker can ultimately evade, if he or she persists. There is a possibility therefore that we moderns have been introduced by cultural changes, not by our own spiritual progress, to a level of truth that only contemplatives and esoteric initiates could bear in the past. I do not think we can bear it ourselves unless we join them on their spiritual path.[6]

The position of the modern person, placed involuntarily by cultural change in a night of the intellect as dark as the classical nights of the contemplative, is certainly an unenviable one. We lack the support which traditional religious structures could offer to the contemplative during this barren phase of the journey. Moderns are therefore very much susceptible to the pressures of the inner voices telling them to give up on the search, to accede completely to the desacralization of the universe, and to rely on technology and material satisfactions, or to embrace existential absurdity. Each of these routes has been rather fully explored in the twentieth century. I believe, however, that it is not premature to claim that something is beginning to emerge into our corporate consciousness as a result of this exploration of false trails. At least two things are becoming evident to an increasingly large number of people. The first of these is a confirmation by our modern experience of an ancient finding: even under the astoundingly rich material conditions of modernity, life on this planet remains deeply unsatisfying. As the Buddhists say, it is characterized by dukkha. I take that to mean, not that we suffer continuously, still less that we should expect to do so as a condition of being alive, but that all the promised satisfactions of our existence, including those which the modern world so abundantly provides, do not, even cannot, deliver what we most long for. And this would be found to be true, and is being found true, quite apart from the disastrous side-effects of a technological culture, such as the pollution of the atmosphere, the poisoning of the earth by pesticides, the over-population of the planet by masses of people living in increasing poverty, together with the overhanging and steadily growing danger of thermonuclear holocaust.

Even if these problems could be overcome, and it is premature to conclude that they cannot, the heart of man would remain deeply unsatisfied. What the modern world can deliver, even when it functions best, is not enough for an increasing number of people. And it turns out that this dissatisfaction is not, as was previously thought, the outcome of neurotic incapacity for enjoyment, but the manifestation of a hunger arising from the depths of our being, which no gratification of our passions and material desires can assuage. We might translate dukkha, then, as something like existential dissatisfaction, and conclude that modernity has actually confirmed, rather than invalidated, the Buddhist finding that samsaric existence is characterized by this dissatisfaction.

The other side of dukkha is hunger for Being, though this is not a Buddhist way of talking. This is the second finding from the modern experience. Even in the collapse of the transcendence of Being, even in the dark night of the death of God, man's hunger for Being persists. We would not experience samsaric existence as <u>dukkha</u> if we were not in need of something more than it can offer us. For the most part, this hunger is experienced as pain, not fulfilment, but it is there, and more and more people are becoming aware of it. Only Being can satisfy this existential hunger. More and more people are therefore returning, in one form or another, directly or indirectly, to this search for Being.

Sometimes we find it expressed in a new attitude to nature, new at least to Western man, in which human beings experience themselves as part of nature, instead of being over and above it and therefore entitled to exploit it for their own purposes. This perspective, in which man is seen as having a place in a vaster eco-system that imposes its own limits on predatory activities is, I believe, spiritual as well as scientific. It has few or no roots in the Christian tradition; it is rather reminiscent of some features of an Asian religious outlook, though precedents can also be found in Jewish tradition.

It has often been suggested that contemporary people turn to the arts for what their predecessors found in religion. If so, perhaps they sense an intimation of Being in the works of musicians, painters, sculptors, poets and novelists, as well as sometimes in their own creativity. They can no longer find such an intimation in the tattered remnants of religion.

The most obvious symptom of hunger for Being, however, is the attraction of Eastern spiritual disciplines, with or without their traditional mythical and metaphysical framework, for many highly modernized Western people. Sometimes these disciplines are being practised in association with certain forms of Western psychotherapy. As Jacob Needleman has rightly pointed out, this "therapeutic" approach characteristic of our own culture does not always lead in a spiritual direction.[7] It often aims at happiness, or adjustment, within the terms of the ego and of ordinary reality. When this occurs, the search of Being is temporarily or permanently aborted. But -- at least in my own experience -- this is not always what happens. Certainly the use of such methods for the purpose of gathering experiences is widespread, especially in the human potential movement. Then the use of such disciplines only serves to inflate the ego. However, there are forms of psychotherapy that deliberately aim at the transcendence of the ego, even by adapting existing therapeutic techniques for this purpose. Such is the case with the post-psychoanalytical psychotherapy practised by my colleague and co-author Ian Kent. Yoga and meditation fit in very well with such psychotherapy, and rediscover themselves in their traditional meaning, if not in their traditional context.[8]

Needleman has also acutely suggested that many, even perhaps all, of the basic insights of modernity can be regarded as esoteric truths divorced from their initiatory context.[9] If so, it would not be surprising to find, as we do, that generally speaking exoteric religion seems to be in a bad way in modern cultures, vigorous only when it is most reactionary, while spiritually oriented people seem to be more attracted to various versions of the older esoteric paths. These paths have become somewhat more accessible at the same time, because they have emerged from their traditional secrecy in response to contemporary developments, and in some cases have been adapted to the needs of Western people. From this angle, the implication of what I have been saying is to agree with Needleman that modernity has evolved in an esoteric direction while losing its contact with the traditional religious world in which such insights formerly belonged. But this in turn means that great numbers of people have been plunged into a form of spiritual experience for which they had not been trained by previous participation in a healthily-functioning exoteric tradition. This experience has left many disoriented and lost. However, looking at things in this way may also suggest a possible way forward, at any rate for some.

Would it be possible to accept and build upon the esoteric character of the modern worldview, since in any case we appear to have no alternative, while at the same time attempting to restore the lost connection of its insights with their original initiatory meaning and function? Maybe that is what people are doing without necessarily thinking out all the implications when they try to satisfy their hunger for Being by using spiritual disciplines that originated in an esoteric context, without giving up their residence in our modernized culture. Surely something like that is going on at the level of popular mythology in such movies as Star Wars where a pop spirituality which certainly has esoteric roots is set in the context of romantic and spectacular science fiction, instead of traditional religion. There can be no doubt that this extremely modern mixture appeals to very large numbers of people. One can find the same thing in a much subtler form in the novels of Ursula Le Guin, and in many other writers.

I believe we can also find in many of these writers, and often in the scientists on whom they depend, an almost mystical feeling of the universe as revealed by modern physics. We do not hear any mention of God in such writers, but there is often an awesome sense of a great

Spirit permeating the utterly astonishing world being presented to us by physicists and astronomers. I do not quite know how to say this, because both our traditional religious and our scientific language are ill adapted for the purpose. It appears to me that the world disclosed by the most recent science is becoming a mythological code replacing that of traditional religion, but performing the same function of opening up higher levels of awareness, given the presence of the necessary disciplines of consciousness. Perhaps this is the standpoint from which we should evaluate such a book as Capra's Tao of Physics. I am suggesting, therefore, that the esoteric insights of modernity which are part of our own outlook could be used instead of rejected, and even turned to our spiritual advantage.

It does not seem likely, accordingly, that the spiritual condition of modern man will lead to a return to religion in any traditional sense. Unless a new, non-modern culture arises, presumably after the catastrophic collapse of our own, the great religions of revelation will not find a fertile soil to flourish in. Modern spirituality, if it exists at all, is inevitably esoteric in character, because the foundations of modern culture are themselves esoteric in their spiritual implications. Even the choice of adhering to what is supposed (wrongly) to be a traditional orthodoxy is really a form of low-grade esotericism, like belonging to a fringe order of Sufis in an Islamic country; such a group practises piety with regularity and intensity, but knows little or nothing of the classic initiatory disciplines. Modern man is far more able, I believe, to respond to what I have termed "immanent transcendence." Although we are perhaps no longer open to the older experience of exterior transcendence, built upon the mythological idea of God as king sitting exalted on the throne of the universe, we may become aware of being responsible for our own truth and authenticity through our inner capacity for discrimination and self-transcendence.

This may lead us to a further question. Since modern culture proclaims itself to be based on science and not on dogma (though in practice many scientists unfortunately behave very dogmatically), is it possible to conceive of an empirically based spirituality, which (like science) tests its theories against reality? Can we in any sense speak of spirituality as a scientific pursuit? I believe we can, provided we admit from the outset that there is no possibility of quantification in this domain. If a quantitative approach is essential to all scientific disciplines, as it certainly is to all the hard sciences of today, the answer is clearly no. We can't quantify contemplation or love. But if the essence of science is trial and error, learning from our mistakes, allowing reality to feed back to us a correction of the idea with which we approached it, the answer is surely an equally clear yes. We could even argue that this is one of the differences between esoteric spirituality and socially constituted religion. Even with the presence and assistance of a spiritual guide, spirituality is a do-it-yourself affair. We have to be willing to try something, if necessary make a mistake, and learn from it to correct our path. In this sense, as a few of our colleagues in psychology are beginning to realize, the spiritual classics of various cultures are psychological texts, though also more than that. Through such experiental approaches to the spiritual domain, much has been learned about man, and about the laws of spiritual life, which has stood the test of time. The findings of the pioneers have been replicated by their successors, and a body of knowledge has been built up.

However, at the present time I am much less impressed by any supposed need for spirituality to become quasi-scientific, perhaps in alliance with new psychologies and psychiatries (which is happening in any case), than I am by the urgent necessity for the reunion in all disciplines of the logical-analytical intellect with feeling and intuition. As we saw at the outset, the modern mind is not just the intellect liberated from religious restraints and limitations, it is also the intellect divorced from intuition and feeling. Such a divorce or division may be appropriate in the pure sciences, though even there we are frequently reminded of the role of imagination and intuition in the making of major scientific discoveries; it is out of place and highly destructive in the social sciences and in the humanities, and above all in the social and intimate interactions of actual human beings. Anyone who says anything like this today is open to the accusation of romanticism, or of nostalgia for the sixties. Perhaps it is important, therefore, to clarify what I mean. I am not arguing for the displacement of reason by emotion. I am simply suggesting that sane human living requires a balance between rationality and feeling, between logic and intuition. The balance will be different in different individuals, according to temperament; but no one can afford to be altogether one-sided. Not only balance is needed, however, but also connection between these two sides of the mind. They should act in concert. Reason alone will not give us wings to mount up into the spiritual atmosphere. But feeling alone, unguided and unchecked by reason, can lead to the occult or to fanaticism. Together they can bring us back from the desert of technological and dehumanized culture to a more fertile soil for the spiritual growth of human beings.

How can this healing of the split in the modern mind be brought about, and whose responsibility is it to foster such a development? If I am right, we cannot expect a return to religion to do it. We shall not see traditional religion again, providing whole societies with order and meaning. The way for individuals and small groups may, it seems, be no more rugged than in the past. The insights on which the modern outlook is based can be used as spiritual stepping stones. But there seems to be no solution here for society as a whole. Yet the fate of society cannot be ignored, unless things get so bad that it has to be judged a lost cause, and individuals put their own personal and spiritual survival on the top priority, as has happened not a few times in the past. Can anything take the place of exoteric religion, by performing approximately the same social functions?

Doubtless no one agency in the modern world can perform all the functions formerly discharged by exoteric religion. We have already noted that some literature and movies are capable of exercising a spiritualizing influence on the popular mind, even in our own culture. But the fact is that, after the home, the schools and universities are now the most powerful socializing influences. It is not easy to affect the home directly, but we ourselves can exert some influence on the educational system, since we occupy positions, in the case of many of us relatively powerful ones, within it. At present this influence on society is being exercised in a way characteristic of modernity in its most destructive form. We are witnessing and conniving at a new "trahison des clercs,"[10] comparable to that which preceded World War II. I do not believe that the conservative critics are mistaken in all their criticisms of public education in North America, especially when they accuse it of propagating a "value-free" ideology which is actually value-laden, but in a destructive way. Their main error is probably believing that they have themselves anything constructive to put in its place. Certainly "value-schools" and creationism are not what we need. Nevertheless, it is true that public education is being increasingly dominated by an anti-humanistic ideology which is almost going by default. Behaviouristic in psychology, socially deterministic in its analysis of society, structuralist or even deconstructionist in its attitude to literature, art, and music, obsessed with technique and methodology to the exclusion of human content, this ideology progressively despiritualizes all who are exposed to it, eroding their capacity to respond with feeling to human beings and human interrelationship. This cold, dead, intellectual world to which young people are being exposed, in the home as well as in the schools, fills them with suppressed rage, driving them to alcohol, drugs, promiscuity, vandalism and violence against people. Only the strongest can survive this scene uncontaminated. We are building up a _damnosa haereditas_ for our society.

Surely it is possible to see this and take corrective action without falling into the trap of conservatism and illusory reaction. Those educators who are becoming aware of what is going on will have to take courage and stand up to it, in spite of curricula and curriculum committees and the suspicions of colleagues, and carve out a place once more in the educated world for feeling and intuition, without neglecting reason. It will have to be done first of all in the humanities, in the study of religion, literature and the arts, and then progressively throughout the academic world, not excluding the faculties of education. This is now a huge task, since so much has been let go, but it is an essential one if our world is to survive as a place fit for children to be brought up in. It can only be undertaken if we educators reconnect with our own spiritual resources, so that we have something to offer to our students, who are searching for the bread of the spirit, and are receiving only academic stones. We can only begin where we are. In religious studies, such a beginning might be made by making a firm commitment in our own writing and teaching to the reality of the spiritual domain, and to the necessity for taking its manifestation in human beings and human life as an object of disciplined study. Without being ungrateful to them for their contributions, we will have to take the study of religion back from the anthropologists and the sociologists and assert our right to say something no one else will say at present, that men and women, modern or otherwise, are inalienably spiritual beings, and that unless this dimension of their being is nurtured, humanity will die and all their cultures with it.

NOTES

1. Cf. Thomas Merton, New Seeds of Contemplation, New York: New Directions 1961, pp. 3f.

2. Cf. Martin Buber, Eclipse of God, London: Gollancz, 1953.

3. I am referring especially to the discussion arising from the publication in 1951 of Dietrich Bonhoeffer's Widerstand und Ergebung, München: Kaiser Verlag; E.T., Letters and Papers from Prison, London: SCM Press, 1953.

4. H.A. Hodges, Christianity and the Modern World View, London: SCM Press, 1949.

5. Cf. Plotinus, Enneads 6. 9. 11.

6. Cf. T.S. Eliot, Burnt Norton I: "Humankind cannot bear very much reality," Collected Poems 1909-1935, London: Faber and Faber, 1936.

7. Cf. Jacob Needleman, A Sense of the Cosmos, Garden City, N.Y.: Doubleday 1975, Chapter 5.

8. Cf. Ian Kent and William Nicholls, I AMness: The Discovery of the Self Beyond the Ego, Indianapolis and New York: Bobbs-Merrill, 1972.

9. Needleman, op. cit. This is one facet of the central argument of the whole book.

10. The phrase is Julien Benda's.

CAUTION! MORALISTS AT WORK

Tom Sinclair-Faulkner

> The acids of modernity are dissolving the usages and
> the sanctions to which men once habitually conformed.
> It is therefore impossible for the moralist to command.
> He can only persuade. To persuade he must show that the
> course of conduct he advocates is not an arbitrary
> pattern to which vitality must submit, but that which
> vitality itself would choose if it were clearly under-
> stood.

Walter Lippmann, A Preface to Morals (p. 319)

Among the participants in this Consultation there was a widely
stated conviction that it was probably the first of its kind, and certainly the first with which the participants were acquainted: a serious
academic effort to "bring together existing and new research on the
effects of modernity on religion from a cross-cultural angle." The
conversation that emerged during the closing hours of the consultation
moved in pathways that were remarkably similar to the way of the
moralist that Lippmann had prescribed fifty years earlier.

It is difficult to cast a neat net around the variety of participants and papers that made up the consultation. The twenty-three
persons who took part were each practising some form of scholarship that
had to do with the study of the effects of modernity on religion, and
each made some explicit reference to their particular work in the course
of the discussions. It became clear that all granted the validity, even
the necessity, of insights grounded in cross-cultural studies from
diverse disciplinary angles, though some participants in practice
approached their studies from only one disciplinary point of view and
with attention to one particular culture alone.

The consultation followed the pattern suggested by the table of
contents of this collection. The first papers introduced a note of
caution, drawing on the perspective of the social sciences to argue that
modernity is difficult but important to define. John Wilson proposed
that modernity is a recurrent phenomenon, not something peculiar to our
era. But he suggested that our modernity is, perhaps, uniquely characterized by a disposition to study religion rather than Christianity,
Buddhism, Islam, etc. Robert Ellwood then set our modernity into the
largest possible historical perspective by viewing it through the

anthropologist's categories of Great Tradition and Little Tradition.

A series of case studies followed, turning the consultation's attention to European racism, modern utopias, Afrikaner religion, a new movement among Japanese Buddhists, the work of professors of religious studies, and Islamic views of modernity. Finally three papers raised philosophical questions about being religious in the modern world.

In the closing hours of the consultation a paradox appeared. In response to a query about the desirability of publishing the papers presented during the event, participants were curiously modest. Yes, the papers had merit; yes, there were a number of avenues to publication; but no one insisted that the consultation must at all costs be enshrined in print. On the other hand the participants were evidently delighted by the conversation that had developed concerning how to live religiously in the modern era. They had cautiously accepted a task that went beyond studying about the effect of modernity on religion, and were undertaking what Lippmann described as the task of the moralist today.

Amid some grumbling that the philosophical papers had been left until the end of the consultation rather than melded with the other papers to promote discussion from the start, the two closing sessions began as a dialogue between William Nicholls and Huston Smith, authors of papers that dealt with the possibilities of transcendence in the modern world. The dialogue soon became a many-sided conversation.

It began with John Wilson's request that Nicholls clarify what he meant by "ecstasy." Nicholls's response was consistent with Lippmann's observation about the acids of modernity, and reflected a widely held view at the consultation. Ecstasy, he pointed out, was a term derived from neo-Platonism, can be achieved by going above, below, or beyond the mind, and entails overcoming the subject-object dichotomy. In other areas ecstasy was achievable through the external working of the divine, but it is in the nature of the modern world that such working is eclipsed. Something else must take its place.

In the conversation that followed Huston Smith emerged as a conservative reluctant to abandon the Great Traditions as means of transcendence, particularly where such abandonment opens the way to a radical subjectivism. When Nicholls advanced the notion that modernity entails a "dark night of the soul" that envelops all who inhabit the culture, I noted that the "dark night" was a technical term from seventeenth-century Christian mysticism that referred to a state into which God hurls religious adepts for further refinement, not something to which everyone, skilled and unskilled alike, may be subjected. This perhaps

finicky demurral led to further discussion in which it became apparent
that there was some common ground between the two main positions.
Nicholls clearly valued elements from the Great Traditions even while he
held out against uncritical acceptance of all their forms. Smith
pressed the argument that those who seek transcendence and who admire
the Great Traditions are under a moral obligation to draw on them in
their quest. "If we do not feed the gods, say the Tibetans, they will
starve." And, one may deduce, so will we.

Nicholls argued persuasively that modernity creates an atmosphere
which has the same effect on everyone as the traditional "dark night"
had on the spiritually adept. He conceded to Smith that the habits of
the traditional adepts which carried them through the dark night might
be useful but he objected that today these habits might better be
esoteric rather than exoteric. Others joined the conversation here and
it became apparent that some participants found little to sustain the
quest for transcendence in the religious institutions ("relics," said
one) of the modern world. On the other hand there were those who found
that participation in traditionally religious institutions was helpful.

Smith continued to insist that in practice most modern individuals
are not able to achieve transcendence by themselves. The Asians were
right, he said, in pointing out that few are able to wander like the
lone rhinoceros, that most draw power from shared relationships and
practices. Nicholls responded that there is power in shared practices
but that not all shared practices are apt to the task of transcendence.
Whether the way be old or new, it must begin with purification and be
genuinely open to transcendence.

This led to a turn in the conversation in which participants
sketched some of the modern avenues to transcendence. In the end there
was broad agreement on three, though none expected everyone to follow
each of the three. First was meditation, whether guided by principles
drawn from a Great Tradition such as Buddhism, from a more specific
source such as the life of the Quakers, or from a characteristically
modern source such as psychoanalysis. Second was "virgin nature." As a
long-time resident of the west coast Nicholls found it natural to speak
of the "sense of the pervasiveness of being" that comes from reflective
contact with "mountains, sky, ocean, birds, energy welling up through
dark trees...." The third possibility came through the world opened by
the study of the physical sciences, particularly at its frontiers and in
a spirit of inquiry fuelled by curiosity rather than by a drive to
control.

It was apparent that the participants were operating in the way that Lippmann said modern moralists must operate. Even Smith's defence of the Great Traditions was based, not upon their intrinsic authority, but upon their demonstrated ability to foster vitality. While the participants generally agreed that the acids of modernity are eating away at traditional habits, they had a more sophisticated view of the past than Lippmann did. They knew that some of those traditional habits were not so efficacious as nostalgia might imply, and that traditions that had been etched by modernity might still be found useful by modern persons. They knew that the Great Traditions were compelled to develop means to distinguish between "lowgrade religiosity" and genuine spirituality, and sought to encourage caution and skepticism among their seekers lest the seekers be too easily satisfied with the direction that their quest took. The modern person, however, lives in an atmosphere of scepticism and doubt which, if it does not first stifle the impulse to transcendence, fosters the wakeful questioning that a seeker requires. No one advocated the exuberant embrace of the "secular city" that Harvey Cox celebrated in the 1960s, but none urged a nostalgic rejection of the modern world as necessarily and completely inimical to religion.

While Peter Berger was unable to attend the consultation, several participants remarked that his concerns and methods were reflected in the standpoint of many others who were there. Participants also demonstrated that they supported a plurality of approaches to the problem of modernity, cautiously aware that our era may have certain unique features to it but that some of its impediments to transcendence are surely timeless. The satisfaction at the spirit of intellectual and even moral camaraderie that found expression in the comments of participants was genuine, but it did not provoke plans for a second consultation, perhaps because the cautious pluralism of the consultation encouraged participants to see their own ongoing scholarly work as promising in itself.

SR SUPPLEMENTS

EDITIONS SR

STUDIES IN CHRISTIANITY AND JUDAISM / ÉTUDES SUR LE CHRISTIANISME ET LE JUDAISME

THE STUDY OF RELIGION IN CANADA / SCIENCES RELIGIEUSES AU CANADA

COMPARATIVE ETHICS SERIES/ COLLECTION D'ÉTHIQUE COMPAREE

Also published / Avons aussi publié

Available from / en vente chez:
Wilfrid Laurier University Press
Wilfrid Laurier University
Waterloo, Ontario, Canada   N2L 3C5

Published for the
Canadian Corporation for Studies in Religion/
Corporation Canadienne des Sciences Religieuses
by Wilfrid Laurier University Press